Feltmaking

BY BEVERLY GORDON

WATSON-GUPTILL PUBLICATIONS, NEW YORK

Copyright©1980 by Beverly Gordon

First published 1980 in New York by Watson-Guptill Publications,
a division of Billboard Publications, Inc.,
1515 Broadway, New York, N.Y. 10036

Library of Congress Cataloging in Publication Data

Gordon, Beverly
    Feltmaking : traditions, techniques, and contemporary explorations.

    Bibliography: p.
    Includes index.
    1. Felt. 2. Felt work.   I. Title.
TS1825.G67   677'.63   79-25701
ISBN 0-8230-1647-1

Manufactured in U.S.A.

First Printing, 1980

Contents

Preface

This book is intended to provide a comprehensive look at felt and feltmaking—its traditions, techniques, and possibilities. Artists turning to felt as a creative medium will find instructions and suggestions for artistic and practical exploration, as well as a portfolio of contemporary felt pieces. The first section of the book provides background information that should help define felt and related products; describe the history of felt and felt traditions; and discuss commercial felt and hatmaking processes. I hope this book will be considered valuable both as a reference and as a source of inspiration and ideas.

ACKNOWLEDGMENTS

I wish to thank, first of all, the wonderful artists listed below, all of whom responded enthusiastically to my inquiries on feltmaking. Without them, this book could really not have been written. I am especially grateful to Beth and Larry Beede, who opened their hearts and their house to me and my family and who helped put this book together in so many ways.

Thank you's are also in order to the following people for their advice and assistance: Joanne Mattera, Elyse Sommer, Pat Spark, Bobbi Houllahan, Lynn Mauser-Bain, Hillary and Stan Farkas, Ceil Coberly, and Warren Hadler. Lynda Lowe Oren helped me contact the proper people at the Hermitage in Leningrad for the Scythian photographs. Nicola Knipe helped me translate the Swedish feltmaking book *Tovning*, by Katarina Agren. Helen LoFaro of the American Felt and Filter Company provided me with information on industrial feltmaking and many photographs. Helena Wright, Librarian at Merrimack Valley Textile Museum, Sue Andrews, and James Wildeman were also helpful with photographs and illustrations. Albert Goldberg of the National Felt Company, Perry Brown and William Becker of the Bacon Felt Company, and Bob Rafferty of the Danbury Hat Company all helped by letting me visit their factories. Jeanne Freer and Gloria Handler provided invaluable help with illustrations.

The artists who helped with this book represent a cross-section of people working across America and, in some cases, the world. They range from beginning students to teachers of the fiber arts. I thank them all: their help was invaluable.

Nancy Algrim, Oregon
Lifcha Alper, Indiana
Rhoda Asnien, California
Lynn Barnett-Westfall, Illinois
Sherold Barr, Oregon
Laura Basanta, Pennsylvania
Thelma Becherer, New York
Beth Beede, Connecticut
Pam Bell, Wisconsin
Gaza Bowen, Maine
Carolyn Bowler, Idaho
Nancy Bowser, Rhode Island
Diane Brawarsky, New York
Jean Brenholz, Pennsylvania
Meg Cantor, California
Susan Marie Cunningham, Connecticut
Anne Dushanko-Dobek, New Jersey
Linda Endres, Michigan
Hillary Farkas, California
Molly Fowler, Connecticut
Ruth Geneslaw, New Jersey
Debra Glanz, Oregon
Suellen Glashaussen, New Jersey
Susan Goldin, New York
Kristy Higby, South Carolina
Linda Johnson, Michigan
Karen Kallen, California
Deborah Kaufman, New York
Catherine Kapikan, Maryland
Betsey Klompus, Pennsylvania
Christine LeMar, Wisconsin
Joan Livingstone, Missouri
Diane Lomen, British Columbia
Gayle Luchessa, California
Marleah Drexler MacDougal, Virginia

Deborah McMahon, Illinois
Cheryl Patton McManamy, Massachusetts
Dawn MacNutt, Nova Scotia
Kristina Markstrom, New York
Joanne Mattera, Massachusetts
Connie Matricardi, Maryland
Lynn Mauser-Bain, British Columbia
Leann Meixner, Michigan
Arlene Mylenek, Michigan
Susan Nestel, Massachusetts
Lynda Lowe Oren, Illinois
Barbara Setsu Pickett, Oregon
Joanne Purkis, Pennsylvania
Debra Rappaport, California
Margaret Rhein, Ohio
Melonie Rufty, North Carolina
Laura Schaefer, Massachusetts
T.D. Semmens, Australia
Pat Spark, Oregon
Bud Stalnaker, Indiana
Georgia Stegmeier, Colorado
Lynn Sullivan, Australia
Roger K. Thomason, Texas
Patricia Townsend, California
Deone Tremblay, Rhode Island
Karen Van Derpool, Washington
Caroline Von Kleeck Beard, New York
Pat Boutin Wald, California
Lynn Reiter Weinberg, District of Columbia
Denise Welch-May, Vermont
Linda Welner, Missouri
Gloria Welniak, Wisconsin
Katarina Eva Weslien, Michigan
Carol Westfall, New Jersey
Pat Williams, Michigan

CHAPTER ONE

The Characteristics of Felt

Felt is a pressed, matted fabric formed by the interlocking of certain unspun fibers, most notably wool. No spinning, weaving, or knitting is involved. Rather, through a combination of heat, moisture, and pressure, each individual fiber becomes completely entangled with the other fibers around it. The tangled mass forms a natural, self-tightening, *felted* mat. Looked at under a microscope [1, 2], felt appears as just such a tangle of intertwined fibers, with irregular open areas.

THE FELTMAKING PROCESS

The same basic steps are usually followed in making felt. First, the raw unspun fiber must be properly prepared. When felt is made entirely of wool, the wool may be washed (it need not be), then loosened or fluffed up so the individual fibers can move freely. It may be combed or carded as well. If fibers other than wool are used, they often require other kinds of preparatory treatment (which will be discussed below).

The second step is to spread out the prepared fiber in a pile of the proper shape and thickness. In the case of all-wool felt, several alternating perpendicular layers of wool are generally arranged on top of one another. This is called *laying the batt* or *blanket*. When felt is made by hand, the batt is usually placed between two sheets of backing fabric, such as canvas, sheeting, or reed matting.

The batt then undergoes a *hardening* process in which water, pressure, heat, and sometimes chemical treatments are applied. Hot water or steam is usually spread through the fiber and it is rolled, kneaded, pounded, or vibrated mechanically so entanglement will occur. It is hardened—felted—when it has formed a solid, fairly dense mass that can no longer be pulled apart. It will have undergone considerable shrinkage at this point.

Fulling is the continued working of the felt to get an even denser, stronger fabric. There is often no dividing line between hardening and fulling. The felt is simply subjected to more moisture, heat, and pressure; by entangling, interlocking, and shrinking even further, it becomes more and more solid. The fulling process can be stopped at any time so long as the felt is hard enough for its intended purpose.

Finishing processes may include shearing, singeing, or sanding the felt surface to make it smoother or, at the opposite extreme, brushing it to make it coarser and shaggier. Chemical treatments of various kinds may also be applied.

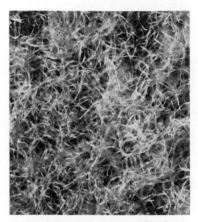

1. Magnified surface view (15X) of commercially prepared wool felt that has been mechanically abraded. The irregular quality and the voids of open space are apparent. Courtesy Merrimack Valley Textile Museum, North Andover, Massachusetts.

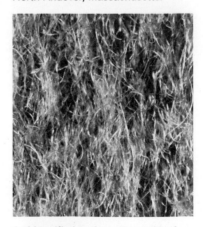

2. Magnified surface view (15X) of commercially prepared wool felt that has been brushed. The same irregular open spaces are apparent, but the surface fibers are all oriented the same way. Courtesy Merrimack Valley Textile Museum, North Andover, Massachusetts.

Why Wool Felts. The question of why wool entangles or felts is an interesting one. Felt was made very early in the history of civilization—at least 3,500 years ago and probably a good deal earlier than that—but the reasons *why* wool felts were not really understood until quite recently. In 1868 an American hatmaker named John Thomson commented that the explanation was "a grand secret that [was] a mystery in all ages, until within a few years." In Thomson's time the answer to the secret was thought to lie in the scales that surround the wool fiber in an overlapping fashion [3]. The theory was that when the fiber was subjected to felting conditions of heat, moisture, and pressure, the scales would swell, open up, and latch on to and hold one another in a ratchetlike fashion.

It is true that wool scales do swell in this way, but felting is actually more complex and interlocking scales do not by themselves explain felting. The way the scales affect the *movement* of the fibers is, in fact, more crucial to the felting process. The scales are fastened at one end (the root) and free at the other (the tip) [3]. The tips of the scales, furthermore, all point to the top of the fiber, giving it definite direction or orientation. Thus, the friction or resistance between two fibers is greater when the fibers are rubbed *against* the scales (from tip end toward root end) than when rubbed *with* the scales (from root end toward tip end). Consequently, a fiber rubbed along the direction of its axis tends to move in the direction of its root end. This phenomenon is called the *directional fiber effect*, or D.F.E.

As many fibers move simultaneously in this backward, root-end direction, they slide into one another and, since they cannot move in the other direction, become irreversibly entangled. Once the tangling has taken place, the friction caused by the scales rubbing against each other helps lock the tangles together. In this sense, the 19th-century theorists were correct.

There is evidence that the wool's *crimp* also affects felting. Crimp refers both to the kinking tendency of the wool and to the actual kinks of an individual wool fiber [4]. The relationship between crimp and felting was addressed in an article written during World War II, when much textile research was undertaken (the following excerpt appears in Niran Bates Pope's *Everybody Uses Felt*). The article, "Washable Woolens for the Army," states:

> In virgin wool, the inner core of the fiber is in a stretched condition supported by the outer cortex. It might be compared to a stretched rubber band coated with sufficient cellulose acetate to support it in the stretched condition. Under the condition of heat and moisture, and lubrication and swelling agents such as soap and alkali, the outer supporting layer becomes plastic, releasing the elastic core and thus causing lengthwise contraction. Because of the uneven forces, the fiber does not contract in a straight line, but much like a bimetallic strip, tends to curl into a tangled mass. The entanglement of many such fibers results in the phenomenon known as shrinkage or felting.

This contraction occurs simultaneously with the entanglement caused by the D.F.E. and the rootward movement of the fibers. Because the crimp of the wool fiber contributes to the felting process, it is generally true that small, short, soft scaly wools (usually more highly crimped) felt more easily than long, large, smooth wools.

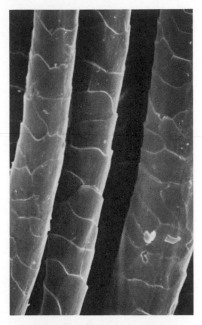

3. Microphotograph of wool fibers. Note the overlapping scales and the orientation of the fiber (the root end is at the bottom). Courtesy Western Regional Research Center, U.S. Department of Agriculture.

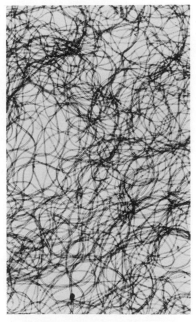

4. Wool's natural crimping and tangling properties are well illustrated by this microphotograph of uncarded wool (20X). Courtesy Merrimack Valley Textile Museum, North Andover, Massachusetts.

I have mentioned that fibers other than wool can also be felted. The soft undercoat or "down" of such animals as the camel, goat, and llama, for example, have a somewhat similar structure and will entangle in a similar way. Their felt will generally not be as firm and as strong as wool felt, however, for the fiber structure is not as ideally suited to felting. These fibers are often mixed with wool, though, and the combination makes quite satisfactory felt.

The soft undercoat of other rodentlike animals, such as rabbit, beaver, and muskrat, can also be used. Felts of this type are classified as fur felts. Fur fibers are first treated chemically (*carrotted*) to allow them to felt: an oxidizing agent is applied to the tips of the fibers, causing them to soften and curl up in much the same way as the wool fiber described above. The root portions of the fur are not treated, for the fur must also move in a root-end direction in order to entangle properly. Fur entanglement is not as thorough as wool entanglement; it is more a semiplastic adhesion of fibers than a true interlocking.

Vegetable and synthetic fibers will in some cases intertwine, but they will not felt by themselves. They can be added as filler—the wool entangles around them—but they do not add anything but mass to the felt. However, the felting tendency of wool is so strong that as much as 75 to 80 percent of a finished felt can be made of filler material. There are also fabrics and products made from vegetable and synthetic fibers that are closely related to felt, including paper, bark cloth, and nonwoven fabrics. These will be described more fully below.

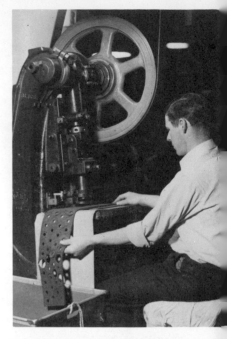

5. Automatic die-cutting machines punch out washer rings in thick sheet felt. Courtesy American Felt and Filter Company, Newburgh, New York.

THE PROPERTIES OF FELT

Felt is in many ways a unique and special fabric with an unusually wide range of interesting, useful properties. In some respects, the properties of wool felt are the natural properties of wool itself, but in other ways the matted structure takes on its own characteristics.

The continuous random entanglement of felt fibers means that there are no yarn elements as such, and every part of the felt is the same as every other part. Because the material won't ravel or fray, it can be cut or stamped into any shape without sewing or reinforcement of any kind. This is, indeed, unique; no woven or looped fabric can be treated this way [5, 6]. There are, furthermore, no size limitations to felt: if hardened and fulled by hand out of doors (that is, not restricted by the size limitations of floor space or equipment), one piece can theoretically be as big as a basketball court. Felt fabric may also be expanded equally in every direction, since more wool can be added and felted in anywhere.

6. Stamping is used to make all kinds of felt shapes. Note gaskets and washers made from felt of varying thicknesses and the cylindrical wicks. Courtesy American Felt and Filter Company, Newburgh, New York.

Felt's homogeneous structure gives it a number of other interesting characteristics as well. Its dense, tangled form makes it highly resistant to deterioration and wear and, even as it does wear down in thickness, it remains basically unchanged. This means that even if the surface fibers wear away from constant pressure and rubbing, the fibers immediately beneath them have the same structure and are equally strong and secure. By contrast, in a woven fabric constant wear means yarn breakage, weak areas, and, eventually, holes. The dense felt structure is also highly resilient; it can be compressed thousands of times with no damage to the fibers and no change in the fabric.

7. These arctic boot liners, made in 1947, are not only warm but relatively waterproof. Ice crystals that form inside the boot leather but outside the felt can be removed by simply taking the liner out and banging it against a hard surface—the crystals come right off. Liners made today are essentially the same. Courtesy American Felt and Filter Company, Newburgh, New York.

Felt is not highly affected by either changes in temperature or exposure to the elements; it is extremely absorbent of moisture as well. Like a sponge, it can hold many times its weight in liquid (including oils) and is not harmed in any way by saturation. These characteristics also contribute to its ability to take dye well and to be successfully treated with a variety of finishing agents without losing any of its own inherent qualities.

Felt is especially versatile because it is so adaptable—it can be made thick or thin, soft or hard. It can be made so hard, in fact, that it can then be carved, drilled, and even turned on a lathe. It can also be sculpted; artificial hands and feet made from felt are said to be unsurpassed for their permanent elasticity and softness. A booklet published by felt manufacturers, Pope's *Everybody Uses Felt*, likens its adaptability to metal: "Its characteristics for any and all uses can be regulated, very much as the hardness of steel can be regulated by heat treatment." As we shall see in detail in Chapter Three, felt is actually being used by industry as an engineering material, made to order for particular purposes and uses.

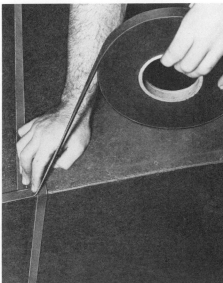

8. Felt insulation was used on the inside of house trailers in the 1950s. Impregnated felt strips are being used to seal board joints here. Courtesy Merrimack Valley Textile Museum, North Andover, Massachusetts.

We can group the uses of felt in general categories, all of which are related to the basic properties of the material. One of the most important is thermal and moisture insulation. In addition to its ability to withstand changes in temperature and moisture, and its resiliency, felt will trap air in its open or void areas, preventing heat or cold from penetrating it. Consequently, felt is a wonderful material for warm garments, as it keeps body heat in and the elements out. Felt boot liners, for example, have been used for thousands of years by people around the world. Their use has actually increased in the Western world recently, for they are commonly found in "snowmobile boots" and are standard in boots made to be worn in the arctic [7]. Felt also serves as an excellent skin for shelter structures [8]; it has been used for centuries in Central Asia as the covering for round tentlike structures called yurts. It has also been used for such diverse purposes as keeping yogurt warm and refrigerated railroad boxcars cool.

The springlike structure of felt allows it to successfully absorb and isolate vibration. Consequently, it is an ideal material for cushioning, padding, spacing (mechanical parts, for example), packaging, and sealing [9, 10]. This absorption capability has proved useful in a wide range of situations: nomads use felt to wrap valuable possessions while travelling; consumers everywhere use it to pad or line their rugs (the felt helps absorb impact and thus appreciably lengthens the life of the rug); footsore walkers find relief for bunions and calluses with felt corn plasters; modern industry uses it to absorb the often boneshaking vibration of heavy machinery.

Felt also absorbs sound and thus has become an integral part of many percussion instruments. We find it, for example, on drumstick tips (beaterballs) and under the keys of vibraphones and xylophones. It is also used in over 30 different places in the piano, most importantly in the piano hammers [11]. When felt hammers were introduced (about 1740), the tone quality of the instrument improved dramatically, for it is the hammer felt, rather than the key lever or hammer mechanism, that controls the amount of percussion by ensuring a uniform impact on the strings. The same tonal quality is thus preserved throughout the musical register. Because the qualities of these hammer felts are so critical, only the most skilled feltmakers can oversee their production. Felt also absorbs sound (and vibration) under noisy machinery such as typewriters and insulates broadcast recording studios from outside noise.

The felt board used by schoolteachers everywhere is a good example of the way the frictional properties of felt can be exploited. One sheet of felt is stretched over a slightly angled board and other, contrasting colors of felt are cut into shapes or letters. These stick slightly to the felt-covered board and can be moved about at will to make a variety of designs or words. It is the surface texture, density, and elasticity of felt that allow it to stick to itself. It will also grab hold of other materials to some extent. Record turntable covers used to be made of felt, for example, because the vinyl discs are "attracted" to the felt.

Some properties of felt have only been explored in relatively recent times with the advent of commercial felt production. Its ability to absorb moisture, for example, is now being exploited in new and different ways. It is excellent for filtering liquids and gases and is used in items as diverse as gas masks [12], oil filters, intravenous feeders (it filters the saline solution), paint filters, and pickle brine filters [13, 14]. It is also used for fluid transfer (wicking) and retention purposes. A popular example of this is the felt-tip pen [15]: felt draws the ink from the reservoir inside the pen, holds it, then transfers it smoothly to the writing surface.

Since commercial feltmakers have been able to carefully control the density of felt, they have also been able to make it hard enough to use in polishing. The felt does not actually do the polishing itself, but acts as the carrier of abrasive particles or grains. When these particles are continually rubbed against a hard surface, they wear away its imperfections and make it perfectly smooth. Felt wheels and molded felt bobs can be made to the proper specifications to polish all kinds of materials, from glass to stone, metal, wood, or plastic [17]. Optical lenses, sheet metal, dental equipment, and fine gems are all polished with felt;

9. Felt pads are used under heavy machinery to absorb vibration and noise and to stabilize the machines themselves. This is a leg of a 6′ high grinding machine. Courtesy Merrimack Valley Textile Museum, North Andover, Massachusetts.

10. A highway worker is installing a ¼″ thick felt strip with an adhesive backing to the angle that supports the grating in the middle of a busy road. The grating itself is 2′ by 4½′ and weighs about 250 pounds. The amount of pressure the felt has to absorb is evident in the piece that has just been removed and is lying on the road (it has been in use only six months). Courtesy Merrimack Valley Textile Museum, North Andover, Massachusetts.

STORY & CLARK PIANO Co.
CHICAGO.
IMPERIAL REPEATING ACTION

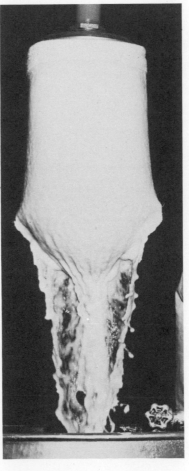

11. (Above) Felt hammers, visible in this open piano, are used to control the percussion and to produce an even sound on all of the strings. Felt is also used in many other places in the piano. Photo Larry Beede.

12. (Far left) Felt can filter out impurities of all kinds. This gas mask is made of pure wool felt, but synthetic felt and nonwoven materials are more common in gas masks today. Courtesy Merrimack Valley Textile Museum, North Andover, Massachusetts.

13. (Left) Felt filter bags are used for filtering a wide variety of liquids— everything from photographic developer to pickles. House paint is being fed through a filter here. Wool, synthetic fibers, and wool-synthetic blends are used in felt filters. Courtesy Merrimack Valley Textile Museum, North Andover, Massachusetts.

  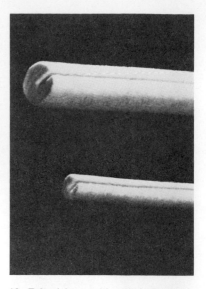

14. A felt filter in the motor of an oil burner. Although this particular model is long out of date, felt is still used in exactly the same way in modern equipment. The spongy, absorbent quality of the felt is apparent. Courtesy American Felt and Filter Company, Newburgh, New York.

15. Felt-tip pens are manufactured from a variety of different felts and with a variety of nibs, each offering a different rate of ink flow and quality of line. Photo Larry Beede.

16. Felt wicks used in office duplicating equipment. Wicks of different diameters and densities have different rates of ink flow. Courtesy American Felt and Filter Company, Newburgh, New York.

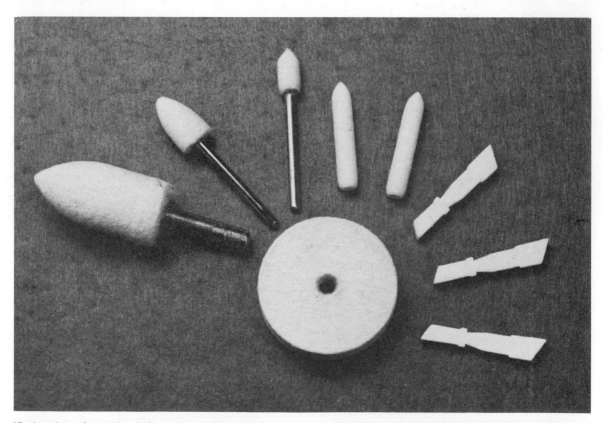

17. A variety of polishing bobs and pen nibs made from sheet felt. The nibs on the far right are made of synthetic pressed felt and, consequently, are smoother and more uniform than the all-wool felt bobs on the left. Photo Steven Vedro.

shoes and floors are buffed in a similar way. Felt can withstand the constant pressure of rubbing against rough surfaces for a surprisingly long time and it ensures even polishing by its ability to absorb large or inappropriate abrasive grains into itself. (Its ability to pick up and absorb chalk grains is what makes it effective in the familiar blackboard eraser.) Felt is also used at times to wipe away waste material and to absorb excess liquid in polishing operations [18].

Felt is now being combined with other materials through the process of lamination. The properties of felt are combined with the properties of other materials for particular purposes. For example, a layer of wool felt can be laminated, or chemically adhered, to a layer of polyethylene (a synthetic film) and used in places where a waterproof material that can absorb vibration is needed.

PROCESSES AND PRODUCTS RELATED TO FELT
There are a number of processes and products, both traditional and relatively new, related to felt and feltmaking. In a few cases both the terminology and the processes themselves overlap, which can lead to some confusion. The following descriptions should help make the distinctions and similarities clear.

Fulling is a term with two meanings. When referring to a step in the feltmaking process, it is the working of the already formed fabric—subjecting it to moisture, heat, and pressure to make it denser and stronger. The word can also refer to a finishing process applied to already woven or knitted cloth. Fulled cloth, like felt, is subjected to hot water and friction, or pressure. In both cases the fibers are made to entangle and the fabric shrink. A fulled woven fabric can be thought of as a woven fabric with a very thin layer of felt on the surface. It has some of the insulating properties of felt, but is generally less dense and more supple and drapable. It withstands abrasion and wears better than an

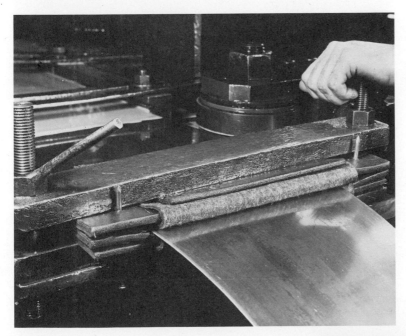

18. A strip of steel is passing through felt finishing pads at a Pennsylvania steel mill. The felt is wiping moisture and chemicals from the steel and simultaneously polishing it. Courtesy American Felt and Filter Company, Newburgh, New York.

unfulled fabric, but is still subject to the fraying and wear of any woven cloth. Most of today's commercial wool fabrics undergo fulling of some kind; cellulosic-fiber fabrics are also fulled in some cases (cotton flannel, for example, is a fulled fabric).

The traditional fulling process in the Western world involved trampling or pounding the fabric, often with hot and cold water, alternately; the addition of alkaline materials; and, sometimes, treatment with an absorbent powdery clay made of finely divided aluminum silicate, which came to be known as "fuller's earth." The clay absorbed dirt, grease, and impurities, and left the fabric with a slightly heavier *hand* (its tactile qualities or feel) and soft sheen. The fabric was then set: generally, it was evenly stretched on a frame between rows of little pegs or "tenterhooks."

Beaten bark cloth might be thought of as the vegetable-fiber counterpart to animal-fiber felt. Interestingly, it is made in tropical or subtropical areas where sheep (and consequently wool felt) were unknown until recent times. As a nonwoven, low-technology fabric, it served some of the same functions in warmer climates that felt served in colder ones.

Sections of the inner bark of trees of the *Moraceae* or mulberry family (most notably the paper mulberry, breadfruit, and wild fig) and mallow family are the most commonly used for beaten bark cloth. The bark pieces are soaked in water and then vigorously beaten with mallets until they soften and adhere to one another. Again, a matted fabric is created, and no spinning, weaving, or knitting is involved [19].

The word "felting" is also used to describe the process of bonding separate sheets of bark and there are many similarities to the process we have been discussing. Several layers of bark strips are repeatedly sprinkled with water, beaten, folded, and re-

19. This Caraja Indian woman from the Rio Tapirape region of Brazil is beating bark for bark cloth. Pounding mallets from all over the world are remarkably similar. Courtesy Field Museum of Natural History, Chicago.

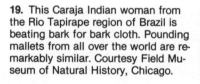

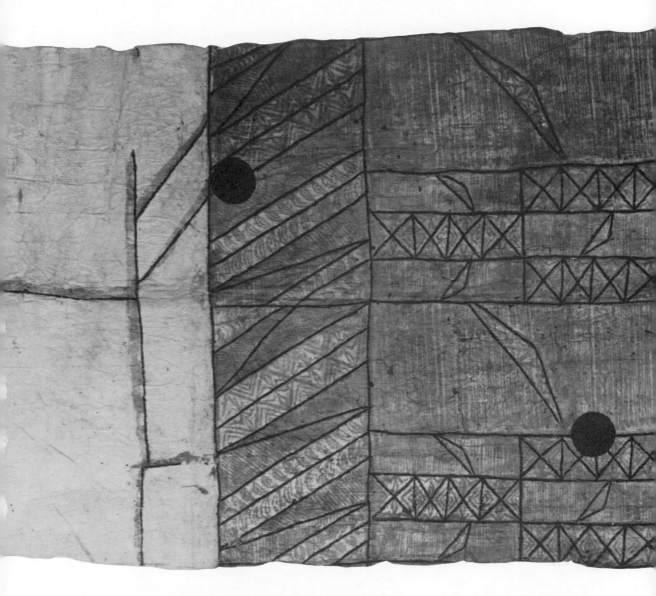

folded until they form one uniformly thick piece. The fibers *do* mesh together, but do not go through a true interlocking process. Instead, the soaking and beating releases a resinous, viscous substance that mats the fiber. In the words of Irene Emery, author of *The Primary Structure of Fabrics*, these plants have "an intrinsic coherence which is retained and utilized; the felting process serves mostly to soften, flatten and increase the native cohesion, and bond one section to another."

Like felt, beaten bark cloth has a homogeneous structure, has no size limitations, and is expandable in all directions. Large pieces of cloth were often made; some Polynesian pieces were as much as 200 yards long. Holes can be patched with more bark cloth, which is usually glued in place with an adhesive made from arrowroot or a similar material.

Beaten bark cloth has been made in essentially the same way in many different areas of the world—Oceania, Africa, Southeast Asia, and the Americas. It is now generally referred to as *tapa* or tapa cloth, although this was originally only the local

20. Section of a piece of Samoan tapa cloth (locally referred to as *siapo*). The fibrous, wrinkled quality of the tapa is visible on the left; on the right are designs that were painted on after the cloth was made. Courtesy Field Museum of Natural History, Chicago.

word for it in Oceania [20]. Like felt, tapa is an all-purpose fabric used in the home for floor mats, sleeping mats and sheeting, room dividers, mosquito netting, and general decoration. Until recently it was also used for clothing: skirts or kilts, loincloths, sashes, wrapped garments and ponchos, and headdresses. Its cultural importance is indicated by the fact that it was used for ceremonial purposes during weddings and other rituals, and by the fact that large bales of undecorated tapa were kept solely to display as a sign of wealth. In most areas, the tapa was decorated—dyed and embellished with multicolor designs that were either stamped or painted on, sometimes with dye-resist techniques.

Other kinds of bark were also used for making cloth. There are reports of fabrics made in northern Europe from lime, sycamore, or birch bark, for example, and the Northwest Coast Indians of North America made extensive use of cedar bark. These trees do not, however, produce a fiber with a resinous substance, and the fibers are interworked (twisted, spun, and so on) rather than felted.

Papyrus, often mistakenly thought of as paper, was actually a beaten fabric made from the *Cyperus papyrus* reed. It, too, was an all-purpose cloth, used by the Egyptians for such diverse items as clothes, mats, sails, and sandals. To make it, the outer covering of the reed was removed and lengths of pith were cut, soaked, and beaten into flat strips. The strips were laid side by side in a contiguous fashion, then covered by another layer of strips arranged at right angles to it. The two layers were then soaked and beaten again. Like the mulberry fibers in tapa cloth, the papyrus fibers worked into one another, or "felted." They were hammered smooth, dried, and polished. The parallels to feltmaking are striking.

Paper is a web made from cellulosic fibers that are suspended in water, sieved, and pressed into a flat sheet [21, 22]. These fibers can be taken from any number of sources: barks, flax, cotton, wood chips, grasses, leaves, rags, or reused paper. The raw material is first mechanically prepared in whatever way might be necessary—cut, cleaned, sorted, and so on—then subjected to a *retting* treatment to separate the cellulosic bast fibers from other unwanted matter. (In plants the principal unwanted substance is lignin, a bonding agent.) Retting may consist of simple water soaking or a chemical treatment.

After rinsing, the fibers are subjected to intense beating and grinding and are broken into a pulp of small frayed pieces. Chemicals may be added at this point for sizing, or for surface qualities such as opacity and color. The wet pulp is then spread over a fine screen in a thin, even layer and the screen is shaken or vibrated repeatedly while the water drains out through the mesh. This shaking causes the pulp fibers to interweave and mat together—to felt, in effect. When the matted sheet is removed from the screen, pressed to remove excess water, and thoroughly dried, the paper is complete.

Other Nonwoven Fabrics. In relatively recent times, the textile industry has come up with ways to produce nonwoven, feltlike fabrics. Because synthetic and cellulosic materials are used in these nonwoven fabrics, they are considerably cheaper than true felt, which usually requires at least some amount of wool. Unlike

21. *The Papermaker*, a woodcut by Jost Amman, is one of 115 illustrations published in a book of trades in 1568; each illustration is accompanied by a poem by Hans Sachs. In the background are a beater (left), which beats the fibers into pulp, and a press (right), which presses excess water from the finished sheets of paper.

wool, synthetic fibers have no inherent tendency to felt, so different manufacturing processes must be used to produce them.

In needle-punched or *needle-loomed* fabrics, mechanical action alone causes entanglement; the combination of heat, moisture, and pressure is not necessary. A layer or batt of fibers is subjected to the action of hundreds of barbed hooks (needles) that repeatedly pass up and down through it, entangling the fibers. As the hooks continue to pass through them, the fabric becomes more and more dense. Density and shrinkage can also be controlled by adding woven material to the batt or making the needled fabric from a mixture of shrinkable and nonshrinkable fibers. In this case, elements of true felting do play a part, for after the needling process is complete the fabric is subjected to intense heat and moisture. Depending on the proportion of shrinkable to nonshrinkable fibers, the fabric will shrink to a greater or lesser degree. Needled felts are generally used for heavy, durable fabrics that need not have any draping properties. One example, increasingly familiar to us, is indoor-outdoor carpet.

Other nonwoven materials use a bonding agent to make the fibers coalesce. Some of these fabrics are very much like paper and are made in the same way, by suspending the fibers in water and laying them on a large sieve or screen. Treatment with a chemical bonding agent usually precedes drying in this wet-process method. In the dry-process method, fabric is formed by compressing batts of loose fiber with heat and an adhesive material. This may be a resin of some sort, or the fibers themselves may be thermoplastic (have a low melting point), which allows them to be shaped or formed when heated. When the batt is subjected to heat, the fibers actually melt together; when it is cooled, they are "welded" into a firm fabric. Some thermoplastic, nonwoven fabrics are spun-bonded, or made from continuous filaments laid down in a directionless batt, which then undergo a heating treatment. Others are made by mixing a small amount of thermoplastic fiber with fibers of a higher melting point. When the batt is pressed through large heated rollers, the thermoplastic fibers melt, sealing themselves into the web. In effect, they become the glue that holds the fabric together. The term "impregnated felt" also describes this kind of material: batts of vegetable fiber are impregnated with a bonding agent and pressed together.

Needled felts and chemically bonded nonwoven fabrics are becoming more and more common. As we shall see in Chapter Three, much of the felt used in industry is now being made either entirely or in part of synthetic materials. We are also encountering nonwoven fabrics in our home environment more often: tea bags, disposable diapers, Pellon®-type fabric interlinings (firm fabric used to add body to clothing, as in shirt collars), and Handi-Wipe® dishcloths are typical examples.

22. Anonymous 17th-century woodcut, reproduced in Dard Hunter's *Papermaking: The History and Technique of an Ancient Craft*. The hats these papermakers are wearing are probably made of felt.

CHAPTER TWO

Felting through the Ages

There are several similar, recurring legends about the discovery of felt. In one, Noah attempted to make his ark more comfortable by padding the floor with sheep's wool. By the time the journey of 40 days and nights had passed, the loose wool had turned to a matted fabric—felt—by the pressure and moisture the animals had subjected it to.

Another legend placed the discovery in France in the Middle Ages. A monk who lived in the city of Caen decided to make a pilgrimage to a distant shrine. He set out wearing a pair of new sandals and his feet soon became sore and tired. To make them more comfortable, he picked some wool from the backs of passing sheep and put it in his sandals. When he arrived at his destination after 15 days of walking, he found a strong soft cloth had been created by the constant moisture and pressure of his feet. This monk is referred to both as St. Clement and St. Feutre (*feutre* is felt in French).

An almost identical story takes place in the Middle East, where a tired, footsore camel driver took some of the soft hair from his camels and put it in *his* sandals. By the time the caravan had reached its destination, he, too, had discovered felt.

THE ORIGINS OF FELT

In actual fact, felt is an extremely old material—many scholars feel feltmaking may predate spinning and weaving. It is impossible to prove anything about the earliest origins of felt, but it is generally believed that it was the nomadic people of Central Asia who first learned to make it. Felt could only be made, of course, where sheep were abundant, as they were on the Central Asian steppes. (It was never made in tropical areas, in Africa, or the Americas.) Felt was, furthermore, an absolutely fundamental element in the lives of these nomads. They used it not only for shelter, clothing, and other necessities, but for religious and ceremonial purposes as well. In other areas it was adopted for utilitarian purposes, but was never as much an integral part of the culture.

The oldest pieces of felted fabric to have been found date from about 1500–1000 B.C. Felt caps as old as 3,500 years have been found in Scandinavia and several items from the later Bronze Age (1400–1200 B.C.) have been found in tombs in northern Germany and Siberia. The pieces have survived in these northern areas because the frozen conditions in the burial

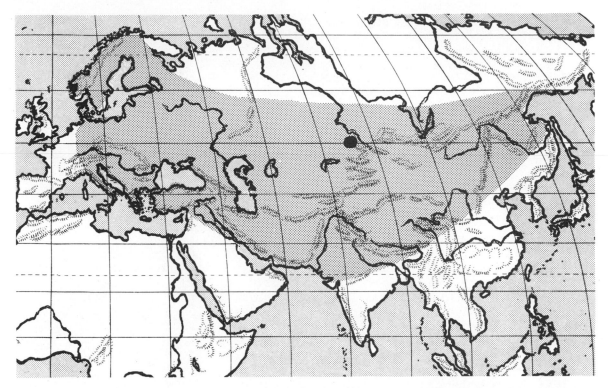

grounds helped preserve them. There is every reason to believe, however, that felt was also made in the more temperate regions by this same date. Because the pieces represent a highly developed feltmaking technology, furthermore, it is probable that the traditions had been carried on for hundreds of years by that time.

FELT OF THE IRON AGE: THE PAZIRIK TOMBS

The Scythians were a tribe of nomadic horsemen and herdsmen who, in the first millennium before Christ, dominated a huge area of Eurasia—as far east as Mongolia, as far west as the Danube River, and as far south as the Tigris-Euphrates valley. Due to a fortunate accident of circumstance, a large number of their artifacts remain in perfect condition: in some of their tombs the objects were solidly frozen in ice; when unearthed in the 20th century they had suffered no decay.

The burial site that provides us with the most information is in the Altai Mountains near Pazirik, at the Yan-Ulaghan River. It is made up of *kurgans*—underground wooden chambers covered by a mound of stones on the earth's surface—dating from about 500 B.C. As we might expect from a sheepherding people, many of the objects in the tombs are made of wool. Superbly crafted wool felt items are especially numerous.

Felt was produced in many grades and qualities, the finest of which was thin but dense and so well controlled and even it approximates today's manufactured novelty felt sold in dimestores. Natural white, brown, gray, and black shades were juxtaposed with vegetable- and mineral-dyed blues, reds, and yellows. Felt was used by itself or in conjunction with other materials—leather, fur and horsehair, gold leaf and tinfoil—for a variety of practical and decorative purposes.

23. The shaded area on this map represents the approximate extent of indigenous feltmaking in the period before the Crusades. Hatmaking traditions were later carried into Western Europe. Apparently, no felt was made in the Western Hemisphere. The Scythian burial site at Pazirik in the Altai mountains is indicated by the black circle at the southern end of the Yan-Ulaghan River.

Kurgan floors were covered with plain, thick felts (usually black), which served as insulating carpets. These plain felts were also used as coffin liners or mattresses and as blankets. Walls and ceilings were covered by huge felt hangings that were generally more elaborate—often appliquéd with multicolor designs. On one set of hangings, for example, a dark brown ground was set off by borders consisting of a band of white between two bands of white, red, yellow, and blue dogtooth patterns. The same dogtooth pattern was also used on both sides of a row of lion's heads in a central band of the same hanging [24].

In addition to regular appliqué, the Scythians used a kind of reverse-appliqué technique. Pattern areas were cut out of the top felt and another, different-colored felt was placed behind it and allowed to show through. Sometimes designs were made using both positive and negative patterns in the same piece. Hangings of this type were apparently also used to cover the walls and roof of the wagons that women and children travelled in as they moved across the land. In both appliqué and reverse-appliqué pieces, sewing was done with fine sinew or woolen thread.

Felt clothing was also found in the tombs: pointed felt caps; stocking-boots of soft but fairly thick felt (most were white with multicolor border and all had a back seam and sewn-on leather sole); a caftan of double thicknesses of very thin, white felt with a fleece band and a lining of small, patched-together felt pieces; a woman's sleeveless cloak edged with fur and covered entirely with appliqué; and bonnets and headdresses that had been molded over spherical wooden blocks.

Felt was also extremely important for saddles and other horse trappings. The saddle, of course, was one of the mainstays of Scythian nomadic life [27]. Most saddles were made of two felt cushions or pillows stuffed with horsehair or staghair and mounted on a central felt or wooden "sweat" band. The cushions were usually covered with enormously complex patterns in felt or leather appliqué [Plate 1]. Sometimes even ornate saddle cushions were covered once again with black, blue, white, or red felt cases; in addition felt saddle cloths fit under the saddle itself. Horse headdresses and mane covers were also made either partially or wholly of felt [28].

Felt entered into Scythian ritual life, too. People taking part in a burial, for example, first underwent a purification procedure, described by Herodotus (and reprinted in Laufer's "Early History of Felt") as follows:

> [After cleaning themselves they] make a booth by fixing in the ground three sticks and over them woolen felts, which they arrange to fit as close as possible; inside the booth a dish . . . of red stones . . . and creeping under the felt coverings, [they] throw some hemp seed upon the stones; immediately it smokes, and gives out [strong] vapours [which they inhale].

Clearly, felt was invaluable to these people. They exploited its insulating properties, its versatility, its moldable nature, and its many decorative possibilities, in all cases demonstrating an enviable degree of control and understanding of the medium.

FELT IN THE LIVES OF THE NOMADS

The Scythian tribes (and others like them) left behind a feltmaking tradition that was carried on by their descendants. In the

24. Scythian lion's heads in blue and red from a set of felt wall hangings found in the Pazirik tombs. Illustration Jeanne Freer.

25. Design of a Scythian lion from a felt wall hanging found in the Pazirik tombs. The designs in the lion's body are indicative of the X-ray style, where the internal organs of the animal are visible. Illustration after Tamara Talbot Rice.

26. Simplified version of a Scythian felt rug with appliqué designs. Scythian motifs tend to be symmetrical and rugs were made with all-over, repeating patterns. Illustration Jeanne Freer.

27. (Top) Fragment of a saddle covering with an appliqué griffin figure. Courtesy The Hermitage, Leningrad.

28. (Above) An elaborate Scythian horse headdress made of felt and leather. The warm felt "hood" on the bottom of the headdress is trimmed with gold foil. The goatlike figure in the center Is made of leather; the bird on top is felt. Flat felt was cut, shaped, stuffed, and stitched together to form these figures. Illustration Jeanne Freer.

29. Scythian stuffed-felt swan from the fifth Pazirik tomb. A swan like this travelled across America in 1975 in the exhibit "From the Lands of the Scythians—Ancient Treasures from the Museums of the U.S.S.R.," which made an indelible impression on many who saw it. The body is white, the wing tips black, and the tail red. Courtesy The Hermitage, Leningrad.

Central Asian area, roughly including Turkey, Afghanistan, Iran, Mongolia, and Chinese and Russian Turkestan, felt continued to play a vital role in the lives of the people. In particular, it was one of the mainstays of nomadic civilization; so much so, in fact, that the Chinese came to call the nomadic territory of the northern steppes "the land of felt," and Genghis Khan referred to the nomads themselves as "the generations that live in felt tents."

The Mongolians not only lived in felt houses (similar to present-day yurts, discussed below), but also travelled in similar structures—round wagons or carts covered with felt that had been soaked in tallow or ewe's milk to make it waterproof. They wore felt clothing—boots, outer garments, and hats—which offered good protection against sun and rain [30]. Felt was even

30. (Above) Although they dress as Westerners in other ways, the nomadic Kashgai men of Iran still wear their traditional hats. Always made of natural white felt, the hats can be worn with both visors up, or with one visor pulled down as a sunshade. Illustration Jeanne Freer.

31. (Left) This bag lined with felt and containing two felt figures belonged to a Barak shaman and was collected in Urte-in Gol in the Chahar district of Inner Mongolia in the 1930s, 15″ x 11″ (38 x 28 cm). The figures are probably direct descendants of the felt idols used by the nomadic people at the height of the Mongolian empire. Courtesy Department of Ethnography, National Museum of Denmark, Copenhagen.

32. (Above) Some of the motifs on this early 20th-century mosaic rug from eastern Turkestan are strikingly similar to those on the recent rug from Afghanistan [33]. Illustration Jeanne Freer.

33. (Left) This felt rug was made in Afghanistan in 1970, 60″ x 135″ (152.5 x 346 cm). The designs were cut out of large pieces of felt and sewn together to form a felt "mosaic." Colors are dark brown, white, dark red, orange, and blue. Courtesy Royal Ontario Museum, Toronto.

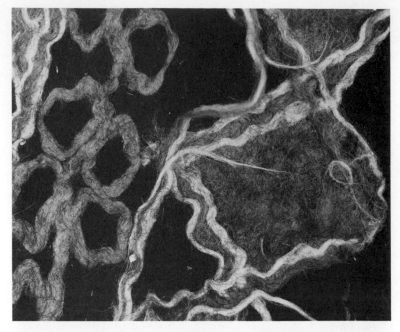

34. Detail of a felt rug with an inlaid design, made in Afghanistan sometime during this century. The background is brown; the foreground decoration is red, blue, and white. Note that the decoration is made of long wool sliver rather than loose carded wool. Courtesy Royal Ontario Museum, Toronto.

35. A Turkoman yurt. Tightly lashed felts are visible on the roof, but the side felts and "skirts" are covered by reed matting. The wooden door is covered by a felt panel, decorated with a design laid directly in the felt. Illustration Gloria Handler.

used during the coronation ceremonies of the Mongolian Khans. The Khan was placed on a mat of white felt and lifted in the air by several attendants, signifying his authority over men but necessary obedience to the gods. Even today Mongolian brides are seated on white felt mats during their wedding ceremonies, and people going on long trips may be given a send-off on white felt.

Felt was also part of the daily religious life of the Mongolian people. In each home, felt idols made by the women were an integral part of the daily routine [31]. As Giovanni de Piano Carpini, an Italian ambassador to the Mongols in 1246, described it (reprinted in Laufer's "Early History of Felt"):

> They have idols made of felt in the image of a man, and these they place on either side of their dwelling; and above these they place things made of felt in the shape of teats, and these they believe to be the guardians of their flocks . . . Whenever they begin to eat or drink, they first offer these idols a portion of their food or drink [by smearing meat, drink, and milk on their mouths].

In addition, they hung one felt idol, which they referred to as "the master's brother," over the man's traditional place in the tent and another, "the mistress's brother," over the woman's traditional place. A third idol, the guardian of the whole dwelling, hung between and above these.

Felt idols were also used under special circumstances. They were hung over the bed of a sick child, for example, and were occasionally made to commemorate the dead or a particular emperor. Felt was generally spread over coffins and, on occasion, royal members of the Mongolian empire were buried with their felt tents. When the empire mourned the death of the Khan in 1316, all minarets and pulpits of the mosques of Tabriz were covered with blue felt.

Other tribes closely related to the Mongolians also made extensive use of felt [32]. In addition to covering their yurt-type homes, people such as the Kirghiz and Kazak of Turkey and Russian Turkestan made rugs, door curtains, saddle covers, pouches, bottle cases, hats, mittens, thick shoe soles, mattresses, window shutters, and packing material for items transported by caravan [33, 34]. The Russian Cossack troops used so much of the material they earned the nickname "the felt army."

The Yurt. The most characteristic and most impressive feature of these Central Asian nomadic cultures was, and in some cases still is, the felt-covered tent or yurt [35]. This ingenious structure is so well adapted to its environment it has remained practically unchanged for over 1,000 years. Although now being replaced by more modern structures, it could be found a quarter of the way around the world at the beginning of the 20th century—from Anatolia in the east to the furthest frontiers of Mongolia in the west, and 1,000 miles, north to south. The frame structure was sturdy but light and portable; the rounded conical shape proved extremely stable for an area with strong winds. The felt coverings provided insulation and protection from rain and snow and could be adjusted as the seasons changed: more layers could be used in cold weather, side coverings could be lifted to allow more air circulation in summer.

Actually, the word *yurt* is a misnomer; it can also be translated as "camping place," "homeland," or "domain." The structure has a number of different names, such as *kherga, khedga,* or *iii* in Afghanistan, and *ger* in Mongolia. Because yurt is the term most commonly used in the West, however, I shall use it here.

Simply stated, the traditional yurt was a round, freestanding, wooden latticework structure, 20 to 30 feet in diameter, with a domed or conical unbrellalike roof made of curved poles. The whole structure was covered by a number of large thick felts. The lattice or wall frame was a curved trellis that could easily collapse, accordion style. There was a door-frame opening in the lattice and struts spanned the structure for added support.

Usually, there were two or three general areas within a yurt, including a formal area for men and visitors and another for women and servants. On the woman's side there was often a cradle made of folded felt, which hung like a hammock from ropes overhead. Several pieces of felt were used to form the traditional yurt: two large semicircular pieces covered the top of the vertical lattice walls; one circular or semicircular piece covered the roof (with a flap for a smoke hole) [36]; and four more rectangular or trapezoidal pieces ("skirts") draped over the walls, hanging nearly to the ground. Some groups further covered the felts with large canvas tarps or reed mats. Ropes were used to tightly lash the felts around the structure [37].

The large felts were almost always white at first, but smoke from the fire in the central hearth gradually darkened them. They turned fawn color, then peat color, and finally black. Although creosote in the smoke helped make the felt waterproof, by the time it had become black it was brittle and useless and would have to be replaced. In Mongolia, as far as we know, felt was never washed or dressed for preservation purposes and it generally lasted about five years.

Inside, the yurt was highly decorated with colored wool ropes, brightly painted lattice struts, embroidery, colored decorative bands and rugs, and tassels. The roof felt was usually trimmed with ropes; eight ropes attached to felt patches ran from the smoke hole to the sides. These were functional, lending support,

36. A roof felt ready to be hoisted on a Mongolian yurt. Illustration Gloria Handler.

37. Raising the felts on a Mongolian yurt: the roof felts are positioned first, then the side felts, and lastly the "skirts." The felts for Turkoman yurts in Iran are put on differently—side felts go on before roof felts. Illustration Gloria Handler.

but also decorative—often hung with tassels and ties. The edges of the large felts were all trimmed with wool rope, usually dyed red or mulberry. Bands of felt or woven material edged with embroidery ran around the sides of the yurt and sennits plaited with different colored wools were sewn around the top of the frame. The floor was covered with several decorated felt rugs, usually brown or fawn color. One was cut so as to surround the hearth on three sides; there were also two large rectangular rugs and several smaller ones to cover odd spaces. Typical rug patterns were worked in black, blue, and red and, even where no specific design was used, small bits of color were worked in to the natural-color background. In summer in particular (when fires were infrequent and therefore the decorations less blackened by smoke), the yurt was so "dressed up" it was sometimes likened to a bride.

Making Felt for Yurts and Other Items. Feltmaking generally took place once a year. In most nomadic cultures, the women were completely in charge of making the felt, but it was sometimes a family project; men were particularly called upon to help with some of the more strenuous fulling processes. Felt was made for many different items, but in those years when the large yurt felts were being replaced there was rarely enough wool for anything else. A complete set of yurt felts could require the fleece of up to 190 sheep—the entire flock of a fairly prosperous, nomadic, Mongolian family. For this reason, the size of a family yurt would generally depend on the size of its flock.

The sheep were shorn in both the spring and the fall. It was the second, shorter shearing that was considered best for fine felt; longer wool was used for spinning. The process used in Mongolia was essentially the same as that used all over Central Asia. Because the Mongolians probably learned feltmaking from the Scythians or people like them, we can assume theirs is the same process used thousands of years ago; probably, in fact, the original feltmaking process.

Felt was usually made outdoors in September. A large piece of leather was spread on the ground and covered with the newly shorn wool. The wool was then loosened or teased by a great many people beating it rhythmically with willow sticks. Loosened wool was then separated into small piles or batts.

Next, a V-shaped screen was erected as a windblock and two pieces of old felt—overlapping to comprise an area about two by eight yards—were laid down on the ground. This old felt was called the "mother" felt. It was sprinkled with unheated water and the batts positioned on top of it, usually by a group of six women working side by side. Careful laying was considered vital for good felt, so this step was a painstaking one. A second layer was placed perpendicular to the first, a third perpendicular to the second, and so on. Often layers of autumn (shorter) and spring (longer and coarser) wool were alternated with one another. Water was sprinkled on between each layer.

The whole felt was then rolled tightly, often around a pole firmly trapped inside. The cylindrical package was rolled back and forth a number of times by hand. Wet leather was wound around it and bound in two directions by straps and ropes. Finally, it was saturated again, this time with water poured into the central opening or "mouth" of the roll. Altogether, up to 50

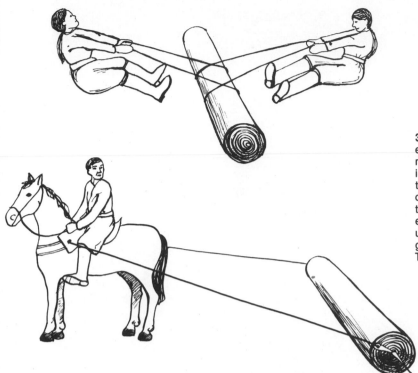

38. Two other hardening/fulling processes used by the Mongolian nomads. Top: two individuals are pulling against one another as they roll the felt back and forth. The holding cords are moved along the length of the roll as they work, so pressure is equal in all areas. Bottom: a horse is used to drag the felt roll along the ground. Oxen were used similarly in Tibet. Illustration Jeanne Freer.

quarts of water might be used for each roll. When the felt was thoroughly hardened, the roll was repeatedly dragged along by a horse in the opposite direction from the one in which the leather was rolled around the wool, allowing the mother and "daughter" felts to separate rather than felt together. The hardened daughter felt was later removed and rolled by itself. The whole process took the better part of the day; the rolling itself might go on steadily for four or five hours.

Other nomads varied some of these steps. Most Mongolians and Tibetans, for example, used mother felts as the base for the roll, but the Turks laid the wool on grass or reed mats or sack cloth, and sometimes used hot water. The Kirghiz and Kazak tribes of Russian Turkestan sized the wool with oil cakes before saturating it with water and layered white wool on top of coarser, cheaper brown wool. The Kirghiz felt roll was pulled by adult women, with a group of young girls following behind, kicking as they went. The mat was removed part way during the process and the felt repeatedly rolled and rerolled in the opposite direction. The Mongolians also worked with partners at times: individuals sat on opposite sides of the roll and pulled on cords [38]. Sometimes the Kazaks formed lines on either side of the roll and kicked it back and forth to one another. Later, they sat down around it and worked it with their hands. Each person would work one section, then pass it on to the next person. Women feltmakers of a Turkish tribe were said to work the roll with their feet in dancelike movements, while chanting songs. The Bashkirs worked a little differently: they unrolled the partially worked felt, folded it in four, and "flapped" it on a bed of planks.

39. Workers in the felt workshop of Cemalettin Özçalişan, of Afyon, Turkey, are spreading the wool batt for a *kepenek* mantle (photograph taken in 1973). Most professional felting workshops are in this kind of dark, airless room. Photo Michael Gervers.

40. The prepared batt is tightly rolled in a reed mat, at the Özçalişan workshop. Photo Michael Gervers.

FELTMAKING IN TURKISH WORKSHOPS

There are also feltmaking traditions among more settled peoples of Central Asia. These people probably learned to make felt from nomadic neighbors, but they developed some of their own techniques for preparing, hardening, and fulling. Feltmaking became an important part of their culture as well and it was early organized into a professional craft for men. In both Iran and Turkey, for example, feltmakers formed guilds at least as early as the 16th century. Although organized guilds passed from the scene in the 20th century, some workshops remain to this day.

In Turkey, feltmakers worked with the relatively clean, sorted short wool from the second shearing. The fiber was usually loosened or teased with a carding bow that resembled a large violin bow, rather than wooden sticks. Made of wood and string

41. The roll is wrapped in cloth and tied tightly prior to hardening. Photo Michael Gervers.

42. Workers in the workshop of Selami Coban, Balikesir, Turkey (1973), are hardening felt by the stepping process. The men bear down on bent knees with their arms, thereby increasing the pressure on the roll. A felt with an inlaid design is visible at left. Photo Michael Gervers.

with several strands of sheep or goat gut plied together, it was similar to the 19th-century hatmaker's carding bow [53]. The feltmaker sat on the ground by the wool, holding the bow just above it, and hit the cord with a wooden mallet. This created a strong current of vibration that moved the fibers and caused the dirt to fall away. The wool was sometimes bowed several times. (Use of this bow, one of the distinguishing features of non-nomadic feltmaking, is less common today as carding machines replace it.)

The loosened wool was then spread on a reed mat with a pronged, rakelike tool [39]. A thick (12–15 inches), loose, puffy layer—likened to clouds seen from an airplane—was formed. Colored designs were often inlaid in the felt by placing strips and patches of dyed wool on the backing mat before the wool ground was laid down. They became an integral part of the felt surface as the piece was hardened.

The wool was sprinkled with water, rolled in the reed mat (several pieces might be rolled in a single mat), and then rolled (mat and all) into canvas or old felt and tied tightly. Hardening was done by stepping, a process that lasted about half an hour [40, 41, 42]. The felt was then unrolled, edges folded under or straightened, and designs adjusted if necessary.

Another layer of loosened wool was usually added to the felt at this point. Water was sprinkled on and it was then rerolled. After this second rolling the fulling process began; hot water and a sizing agent (soap or resin) were added and heavy beating began. This was also the point where separate pieces of felt could be worked or joined together; hoods would be attached to cape-like mantles at this time, for example. In the workshop, the fulling always involved a number of people working together, synchronizing their movements by chanting or singing in unison. The felt was usually rolled and rerolled in every direction. It might also be turned by hand or worked with the knees. Sometimes the fulling was done in a steam bath—especially high-quality felt was produced in this way.

Felt made in these workshops usually also underwent a finishing process to smooth the surface. It was washed, dried, and then polished with a stone, shorn, or singed. Today a pressing machine is sometimes used.

Uses of Workshop-Made Felt. Luxurious, highly refined felts reminiscent of Scythian wall hangings were occasionally still produced as late as the 17th century in Turkey; George Rákóczi, the Prince of Transylvania, ordered some to hang on his mansion walls at that time. In at least one ceremonial yurt at the turn of the 20th century, also, a felt hanging with velvet and silk appliqué was in use. Generally, however, felt made in recent times has been primarily utilitarian—made for and used by working people. Now even utilitarian felt traditions are dying out.

According to Veronika and Michael Gervers, who visited Turkey and Iran in 1971 and 1972 to study felt, there was only one product still made in significant numbers in Turkish workshops. Patterned rugs were made in some areas, but only the *kepenek* [43], the sleeveless mantle generally worn by shepherds, remained truly important. People who worked in the fields still found the felt unsurpassed in the rain and cold. At night the shepherd might even crawl into the kepenek, using it as a sleeping bag.

Other felt products are becoming rapidly obsolete. As the Gervers noted in an article for the *Textile Museum Journal*, by 1972 Turkish and Iranian feltmakers didn't even know what felt-covered yurts looked like and felt rugs were no longer popular.

Associating them with a rural lifestyle and mentality, townspeople scorn them. The felt-makers themselves no longer use felt carpeting in their homes. [They are also now] as expensive to produce (if not more so) as some factory-made rugs. The once popular felt prayer mats are now only used by the aged. Felt saddle cloths are going out with the donkey. Yoghurt warmers made from this material have disappeared completely. Ankle boots, once worn . . . as protection against rheumatism, are practically unkown today, and the knee-length felt boots which until a generation ago were worn by the Turkish army for walking on snow . . . are now but curiosities. Wearing of the felt fez has been strictly forbidden by the Government [since about 1925].

43. The *kepenek* mantle, one of the few felt garments still in use today, must be very heavy on the shoulders. However, as it is also used as a sleeping bag, a lean-to shelter, and for general protection, it is a remarkable structure. Illustration Jeanne Freer.

Since the time of the Gervers' visit, more workshops have closed and felt is disappearing even faster. We are clearly witnessing a time of rapid cultural transition and should be thankful to people like the Gervers for their careful observation and documentation of a dying tradition.

TRADITIONAL HATMAKING IN PERSIA

One other type of Central Asian feltmaking should be discussed. I have mentioned hats, but have not as yet distinguished between the construction of flat felt and molded hats. The hatmaking tradition was well established in Persia several thousand years ago. Laufer tells us that Herodotus described the Persian Magi, for example, as wearing "round their heads high turbans of felt which reach down far enough to cover their lips," while Xenophon reported that the Persian king wore a stiff felt hat and his subjects wore felt tiaras that folded and fell forward.

These hatmakers were also professionals. They usually used brown wool, often mixed with goathair and/or camel hair, that had been degreased with potash, rinsed, dried, and loosened with a carding bow. A circular layer of wool about twice the size of the finished hat was spread over a shallow copper dish, which was warmed by a charcoal fire underneath it. This wool batt was then saturated with water and a thick soap solution and worked with the fingers. While the hatmaker was squeezing the batt, the water and soap continued to heat up. When the fibers began to felt together and harden, a flat cotton circle about the diameter of the hat was put in the center and a second batt of loosened wool, somewhat smaller than the first, placed over that. The edges of the bottom batt were folded over the top batt, saturated again with soapy water, and squeezed until the top batt was also hardened and the two pieces were joined together.

This sandwich was then placed inside another piece of cotton cloth and rolled back and forth, first outside the copper dish, then inside it. The rolling was done with both hands and one foot, and took 10 to 15 minutes of continuous work. Next the felt was unrolled and spread open, the center cotton resist removed, and the opening widened by continued working. The stretched felt at the widened opening would become the rim.

The whole form was placed over a wooden mold and shaped until round and smooth, while the rim (which hung down below the mold) was also shaped. The hat was usually put back in the hot copper dish once more until the desired density and shape were achieved.

The hat usually also went through a series of finishing steps. While on the hat block it was shaved, scraped, and ground with a pumice stone. It was again dipped in hot soapy water, then burnished with wood and another stone. The rim was cut. After washing and drying, it was often dipped in a solution of gum tragacanth and burnished a final time with a stone.

FELT IN TIBET

The Tibetans used felt in many of the same ways as the Central Asians. They did not ordinarily live in felt-covered yurts, but they did use them for special ceremonial purposes. Tibetan chiefs sometimes kept a yurt outfitted for entertaining priests or for religious and state functions. Large felt tents were at times used by noblemen; some were large enough to house several hundred men and were used as military barracks.

Until the Tibetans had extensive interaction with the Chinese, in fact, felt was used widely at every level of society. Everyone wore felt hats—even the Dalai Lama wore the man's traditional, high-crowned, red-fringed hat. Nomads typically wore high conical hats with a downward-turned brim. Felt boots were used by women of every rank; in "The Early History of Felt," Berthold Laufer describes them as knee-high, "trimmed with colored patches, the lower part white, then red and green." They were lined with wool and had heelless leather soles.

Observers agree that one of the most important Tibetan felt items was the large poncho-type raincoat, related in function to the Turkish kepenek. In a study of Tibetan nomads, *Fields on the Hoof*, Robert Ekvall describes it as follows:

> When he rides, it covers him, his weapons, saddle gear and saddle bags, and half the horse; when seated at the campfire, it amply shelters him, his belongings, the food he is eating, and if he so wishes, half the fire on which the food is being cooked; and when he beds down in bivouac, it covers completely his bed and gear.

Laufer commented that when he travelled in Tibet in the 1930s, he found this garment "perfectly safe protection in the most violent rain and snowstorms."

Felt was also used for lining clothing and boots, for rugs, bedding, horse blankets, saddle liners (sweat bands), and saddle pads—generally, the same items found in Central Asia [44, 45]. An unusual use of the material was for plates.

Tibetan feltmaking procedures did not differ significantly from those we have already described. One additional type of felt, primarily used for clothing, should be mentioned, however. Here the fleece was used as it came off the sheep after shearing, without any loosening or carding. The felt produced from this kind of batt tended to be soft, with a smooth face on the shorn side (where the fibers were relatively separate) and a shaggy face on the other side (where the locks had already become entangled with each other before felting).

Due to the current political situation, it is difficult to know what felt products are being made and used in Tibet today. It is

44. Yellow felt pouch excavated by Sir Aurel Stein at Miran Fort in Chinese Turkestan (Tibetan-occupied period, A.D. 750–860). The binding on the edges is buff silk, the strings are red and pink. Courtesy Trustees of the British Museum, London.

45. Shoe excavated by Sir Aurel Stein at Mazar-tagh. The felt is quilted throughout with strong hemp thread, the patches are of leather, and the inside cloth is red wool. Courtesy Trustees of the British Museum, London.

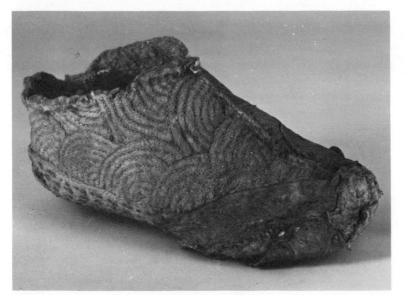

reasonable to assume, however, that some traditional felt items (particularly hats and other protective coverings) are still in use and that there is felt production among whatever nomadic population still exists.

FELT IN INDIA

The felt tradition in India goes back to fairly ancient times; the Greek geographer Strabo tells us felt was mentioned by Nearchus, a Greek admiral who visited India in 325 B.C. Some cloaks, leggings, and other garments were made, but the primary uses for felt seem to have been as rugs, horse blankets, cushions, and bedding of various sorts. White felt was most common, but some was made from a mixture of wool, goat hair, and camel hair, so natural shading was also exploited. Decorative patterns were sometimes inlaid as well.

Westerners may be familiar with *Numdah* (also spelled *Namdah* or *Namad*) rugs, imported in great numbers from India since about 1925 [46]. (*Numdah* simply means felt; there are also numdah socks and hats.) Generally, these rugs are white, relatively small, fringed with felted-in locks of wool, and embroidered with floral designs in colored wools. Interestingly enough, the felt for many of these rugs is made in eastern Kashmir, quite close to Tibet. Descendants of the people who helped produce the famous Kashmir shawls (no longer made today) are now working on this felt. After the rugs are felted, they are shipped by the bale to Srinagar where, according to Enakshi Bhavnani reporting in *National Geographic* in 1951, "needlemen in dark lofts strain their eyes embroidering them."

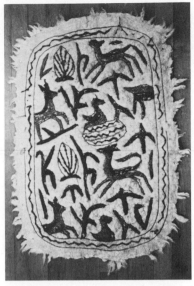

46. Modern Indian *Numdah* or felt rug, embroidered in multicolored wool yarns, 45″ x 35″ (110.4 x 88.9 cm). Photo the author.

FELT IN CHINA

The use of wool and wool products was not originally an integral part of Chinese civilization; it was not until they had extensive contact with nomadic peoples of Central and Northern Asia that the Chinese began to use it. Berthold Laufer, an authority on the history of felt, believes they first came to know the material during their prolonged conflict with the Hsiung Nu, a Turkish tribe of horsemen that lived in yurtlike tents and wore felt coats and outer garments. In 307 B.C. Wu Ling, king of a Chinese principality, adopted some of the clothing and battle habits of the nomads, finding them to be highly advantageous. "Chinese garments were spacious, loose and flowing," Laufer points out, "and a serious obstacle to riding and shooting, while the costume of the nomads was tight fitting and equipped with [practical] boots."

During the Han dynasty (202 B.C.–A.D. 220) mats made of felt were common, though it was still considered a "barbaric" material. This attitude seems to have changed by the fourth and fifth centuries; Laufer remarks that "a certain Liu Ling-ch'u, who lived in the fifth century, . . . is said to have cut human figures out of felt for magical purposes." By the next century, Yüan Siu was coronated as emperor of the Northern Wei dynasty in a felt tent (A.D. 532) and raised heavenward on a piece of black felt during the ceremony. During this period, from about the third to sixth centuries, many nomadic tribes overran and seized much of China north of the Yangtze River. The Chinese were obviously strongly influenced by their Mongolian and Central Asian invaders at this time.

The earliest extant Chinese rugs, dating from the eighth century, are made of felt. These were made in the color-inlay technique, with patterns of brown and blue on a white, gray, or light blue background. The designs are similar to others found in various contemporary Chinese media.

By the ninth or tenth century, felt appears to have been especially important in southwestern China, where sheep were abundant. In 1148, Chou K'u-fei described the people of the southern provinces of Kwang-tung and Kwang-si, indicating that felt was thoroughly integrated into their culture. The felt garments he describes (as reprinted in Laufer) bear striking resemblance to those of Central Asia and Tibet:

> From their chieftains downward to the lowest man there is not one who would not throw over his shoulders a piece of felt. The sole difference between the two classes is that the chieftains wear an embroidered shirt on their skin and don the felt over it, while the common people wear the felt directly over their skin. The felt of northern China is thick and solid; in the south felt pieces are made to a length of over thirty feet and to a width of from sixteen to seventeen feet. These are doubled along their width, and the two ends are sewn together, so that they are from eight to nine feet wide. They take a piece of felt lengthwise and wrap it around their body, fastening it with a belt around their loins. The women follow the same practice. During the daytime they are thus wrapped up; at night they sleep in their felt blankets; whether it is cold or warm, these are never separated from their bodies. In their upper part these blankets are decorated with designs like walnuts. Those which are long and big and yet light in weight are held in the highest esteem.

47. Two variations of the Greek *petasus*. This type of hat was popular with travellers as the large brim acted as a sunshade. Illustration Jeanne Freer.

In later years, felt seems to have been particularly important to the lower classes in China. In 1863, according to S. Wells Williams's *The Chinese Commercial Guide* (cited by Laufer), felt caps were "worn by the poor throughout the whole country. They are of various shapes and different degrees of fineness; some are made hollow so that when pulled out, they resemble a double cone." Rosa Bell Holt, in *Rugs: Oriental and Occidental, Antique and Modern* (published in 1901), claimed people of the "labouring class [in China] use felt [rugs] in their houses. These are cheap and durable, and are placed on the tile floors . . . in the colder parts of the country."

Chinese felt was made in much the same way as Mongolian or Tibetan felt, but somewhere along the line they adopted the carding bow. Describing the feltmaking process in the early part of the 20th century, Laufer remarked that the layers of wool "heaped on a bamboo mat [are] carefully moistened with water sprayed from the mouth in the same manner as our Chinese laundrymen moisten linen."

In 1930, felt caps, hats (including rain hats), coats, shoes, shoe soles and stockings, rugs, carpet bags, and tablecloths were still being made and used. Whether or not these items and the felt blankets of southern China are in use today in the People's Republic of China I have been unable to determine.

FELT IN THE WESTERN CLASSICAL WORLD

Felt was made by the Greeks almost as far back as we have any records. In the *Iliad*, Homer tells us that Odysseus wore a felt-lined helmet; slippers, pads, and capes were made as early as 1000 B.C. We can reasonably assume the Greeks learned feltmaking from the nomadic people of Central Asia; that Herodotus described the Scythians as living in felt tents clearly indicates the interaction between the two cultures.

Odysseus's helmet was only one of many protective devices that made use of felt. There are several references to felt cuirasses or suits of body armor, as felt was particularly helpful in protecting the body from the points of arrows. Wooden towers and military "engines" were also covered with felt, hides, and sackcloth for protective purposes. Aristotle mentions that sheep and other animals were sometimes covered with pieces of felt, again presumably for protection.

Perhaps the most pervasive felt item in Greek life was a close-fitting conical hat usually worn by fishermen and sailors (including, in literature, Charon and Odysseus), and craftsmen. This hat was fairly water repellent and made to be pulled down over the ears for added warmth. A broad-brimmed, low-crowned felt hat called a *petasus* [47] was also popular. Traditionally worn by hunters and travellers, this served primarily as a sunshade.

The Romans learned feltmaking from the Greeks and the tight-fitting Greek cap lived on as the Roman *pileus*, which soon held great meaning for the Romans. The twin brothers Castor and Pollux (representing the constellation Gemini) were so strongly associated with felt that the image of two felt caps and a star was a symbol for the twins. Because Castor and Pollux were the tutelary powers for the middle class, the pileus came to be associated with the middle class, with civil liberties, and, by extension, with freedom. When a slave was freed, for example, he traditionally shaved his head and wore a felt cap. Consequently, the phrase *ad pileum vocare*—"to call to the felt cap"—came to mean "to provoke slaves to rebellion through promises of freedom." Likewise, the common people who poured onto the streets after the death of Nero were referred to by Nero's biographer, Suetonius, as a "felted mob." Two Roman coins illustrate this association between felt and freedom: one, with a cap surrounded by spears, celebrated Caesar's assassination [48]. This was probably minted by Marcus Brutus (one of the assas-

48. The felt cap surrounded by two swords on this Roman coin symbolized the freedom newly won by the assassination of Caesar on the *Eide Mar* (Ides of March). Illustration Jeanne Freer.

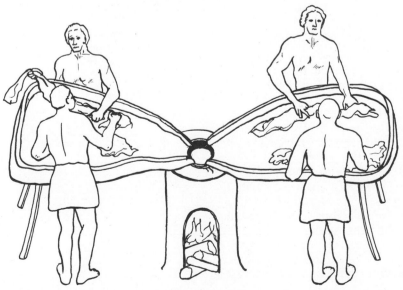

49. Felt being kneaded in a trough of hot water, drawn after a wall painting found at Pompeii. Illustration Jeanne Freer.

sins); his likeness is imprinted on the reverse side. The other, on coins minted during the tranquil reign of Antonius Pius (A.D. 138–161), shows Liberty holding a felt cap in her hand.

Happily, one of the wall paintings that came to light at Pompeii shows a group of men making felt. Stripped to the waist, they stand over a pair of troughs heated by a central furnace, kneading masses of wool [49]. In the same painting, a woman seated behind a nearby counter is selling a pair of slippers to a customer. In addition to hats and slippers, felt gloves, helmet linings, and shoe linings were made in Rome; both wool and rabbit fibers were used.

One fascinating aspect of Roman feltmaking was described by Pliny the Elder in his *Natural History*. He claimed that wool felt ("self-felted fleece") soaked in vinegar was capable of "even resisting iron [alternately translated as steel] and what is still more, fire." Exactly what this means is not clear, but since vinegar tends to open the scales of woolen fibers, presoaked wool of this kind could have made an exceptionally tight, strong felt. In any event, it is obvious feltmaking was highly developed in Rome at this time.

Felt is not mentioned in the Bible or in early documents of the Assyrians, Babylonians, or other people of the ancient Near East. Later Jewish documents do indicate, however, that it was used for clothing, hats, shoes, slippers, and "garments of the dead." Again we can assume the felting techniques ultimately came from the nomadic people of Central Asia.

EUROPEAN FELTING TRADITIONS

Some sources claim the art of feltmaking was lost to Western Europeans after the fall of Rome and until the time of the first Crusades (the ninth century), when they were reacquainted with it from people of the Middle East. This cannot be completely accurate, as the traditions never died out in Scandinavia or in parts of the Mediterranean. Moreover, felt actually came into *greater* general use during the Middle Ages: felt saddle covers and helmet linings were popular once again and felt lance supports (attached to the cuirass) were often mentioned in conjunction with chivalrous exploits.

Generally, though, felt was a low-status material. In 14th-century Italy, Jews were sometimes required to wear a piece of felt on their outer clothing; "penitents" likewise had to wear a (presumably rough) felt shirt next to their bodies.

Felt hats for men, however, became a fashionable exception. Chaucer mentioned them in the 13th century; during the 14th-century reign of Edward II, a brimmed hat similar to the Roman petasus was worn. When Charles VII adopted a beaver-fur felt hat in 1449, the style became firmly entrenched. By the 17th century even poor farmers had taken to wearing felt hats. The style continued until relatively recent times [50].

Felt traditions have existed in Scandinavia for a very long time—caps containing felt dating from about 1500 B.C. have been found in burial mounds in Jutland and North Slesvig, Norway. Felt hats, capes, and saddles are all mentioned in Icelandic sagas, written between A.D. 1200 and 1300 but describing the period of approximately 870 to 1030. Because more felt was made in the northern parts of Scandinavia than elsewhere, it is probable that these people learned feltmaking from their Russian and Siberian neighbors in the far north.

50. We often think of the felt hat as a brimmed top hat, but many softer styles were also common. At top is a beret from France (early 16th century); above, a cardinal's biretta (15th century). Illustration Jeanne Freer.

Feltmaking was particularly important in Sweden, where some women in each district did the felting for their area. They did not have special workshops, but worked in their kitchens, barns, and stables. There were also occasional itinerant feltmakers, who not only made felt but taught the craft to others as they travelled. Hard, firm socks were perhaps the most important felt item. These were used by everyone—men, women, and children. They were warmer than knitted socks and were worn both inside and outside. Lumbermen wore them as bootliners, housewives wore them without shoes to protect their feet from cold floors in the house. In the 19th century, extra-hard felt socks were used as boots—they were even worn outside by poor children who had no shoes and would have otherwise been unable to go to school in winter. Large socks were also worn *over* shoes when it was particularly cold. Felt mittens, more difficult to make than socks (the thumb is not easily formed), were also popular. Usually these were worn over leather mittens; some were even lined with leather. Hand feltmaking still exists in present-day Sweden, but the availability of commercial felt, synthetic materials, and central heating makes it less and less important.

In Norway and Finland felt products are still in use, but felt is only rarely made by hand, as local and Russian factories produce a great deal of manufactured felt. (This was not true in the 1950s; during and after World War II, Norwegian families resorted to cutting up and refelting old hats when wool was not available.) Felt boots and socks are also most important in these countries. Soldiers in the Finnish army still use felt boots with glued-on rubber soles.

Reindeer hair does not felt well, but the Lapps do have a felt-making tradition. Generally, it is the southernmost Lapps who make it, as they have access to sheep.

Most Scandinavian felt was (and is) made over a felting board similar to, but larger than, our washboard. Because Scandinavian sheep tend to have rather coarse, heavy wool, the felt is generally rough and textured.

Some European fulling traditions were extremely close to felting. The Hungarian *szur*, a garment similar to the kepenek, for example, was made from a fabric woven of coarse, long-stapled wool. The fabric was put into alternate hot and cold baths and then beaten in a trough of running water for about six days. The thermal shock and beating produced a heavily matted, feltlike fabric. In Scotland as recently as the 1950s, cloth was fulled or *waulked* by a group of women who sat along opposite sides of a ridged board made of wooden planks, working it with their hands and feet. According to a description of waulking by Mary MacKellar, written in 1887 (reprinted in the liner notes of the record "Waulking Songs of Barra"):

> Shoes and stockings are stripped off, and with petticoats kilted to the knees, they kick the cloth with heart and good will, singing merrily the while, and keeping time with their feet to the rhythm of the song. Soapy suds are kept on the cloth, and the web is continuously turned round to let the waulking benefit each part alike.

Shrinkage was often measured by the number of songs that were sung: blanket cloth was generally finished after nine songs, but cloth for workclothes was often waulked through another nine. The similarity of these felting chants and songs to those of the Turkish feltmakers and the Mongolian nomads is unmistakable.

51. Both men and women of the Salasca Indian tribe of Ecuador wear thick wool-felt hats at all times. According to legend, the Salascas began wearing this hat when they went into mourning for Atahualpa, the last Ecuadorian Inca, who was killed by the Spanish. When new, the hats are extremely stiff and rather uncomfortable; they soften only after many years of wear. Photo Ciel Coberly.

FELT IN THE NEW WORLD

Despite the fact that woollike fibers—alpaca, llama, vicuña—were native to South America, felt was apparently not made in the New World to any significant extent. The Peruvians, who had developed spinning and weaving to a high degree, may have experimented with felt, but no evidence of pre-Columbian Peruvian felt exists.

Felt hats were brought to Latin America by the Spaniards and became a part of native costume early in the 16th century. Special workshops where hatmakers fashioned different styles of hats for the various native groups were established. Felt hats are still very much in evidence in Mexico, where they are worn primarily by men, and in Central and South America, where they are worn by both men and women [51].

Felt hats were not generally adopted by the native peoples of North America, but they remained an essential part of the European immigrant's costume until recent times. Flat wool felt was not used until the invention of feltmaking machinery in the middle of the 19th century.

TRADITIONAL HATMAKING IN THE WEST

Having indicated the importance of felt hats in Western culture, I shall now briefly examine the way these hats were made. The process was generally similar to that of the Persians (see page 33).

Hats were sometimes made completely of wool (often a mixture of noils—pieces too short for spinning—and longer wool), but fur hats were far more fashionable. Beaver (a good beaver hat could last a lifetime), muskrat, and fish-otter fur produced the most luxurious hats, but rabbit (hare, coney, and so on) was used most extensively. It was also not unusual to press a layer of beaver over an already felted hat body of rabbit fur. Seal, mole, fox, nutria, goat, and camel hair (and in the Middle Ages, even cat and dog hair) were used as well. Different furs were mixed with one another or occasionally with wool.

Careful preparation of the fur was quite important. Only the soft underwool was used, which had to be separated from the stiff outer hairs. Furthermore, the thick winter fur of most animals was preferred to the thinner summer coat. In North America, the best beaver felt came from the fur of "old, battered, greasy skins." Indian trappers, according to Leonard Everett Fisher in *The Hatters*, tanned them by pounding in animal fat, liver, and brains. Mary Elizabeth McClellan notes in *Felt, Silk and Straw Handmade Hats* that, after being rubbed with marrow and dried in the sun, five to eight pelts were sewn into the Indian's robe and worn next to the body constantly for several months. After such long interaction between the fur and the heat and oil of the body, the pelts became greasy, soft, and pliable.

As I pointed out in Chapter One, fur and hair will not felt as readily as wool, primarily because the scales are constructed differently. The next step in the preparation of the fur, therefore, was a chemical treatment to open the scales. Because the chemical turned the tip of the fur a carrot orange color, this process was called *carrotting*. Traditionally, nitrate of mercury was brushed on the upper part of the hairs. The mercury did an admirable job of swelling the fur fiber, but unfortunately had disastrous side effects as well when absorbed into the bodies of the hatters. The "hatter's shakes" (mercury poisoning) was described by a contemporary observor (quoted in McClellan's *Felt, Silk and Straw Handmade Hats*) as:

> first affecting the eyelids, then the fingers, tongue, arms and legs, producing a lurching gait, tangled tongue, and addled wits.

Sadly, the Mad Hatter of *Alice in Wonderland* was based on a true prototype [52]. Carrotting agents have changed over the years, of course, and present-day hat factories use a combination of nitric acid and hydrogen peroxide.

The fur or wool was next loosened and mixed with a hatter's bow—an instrument essentially the same as the bow used in Turkish workshops. In the typical hattery, fiber was placed on a

52. Lewis Carroll's Mad Hatter (who wears a traditional fur top hat) was a tongue-in-cheek comment on the mercury poisoning workers in the hatting industry were subject to until the turn of the 20th century.

53. (Left) The hatmaker is about to pluck the string of his carding bow, which, by vibration, loosens and spreads the wool fiber. Great skill was required to form a smooth, even mass of wool by this method. The illustration is from George Dodd's *Days at the Factories* (1843). Courtesy Merrimack Valley Textile Museum, North Andover, Massachusetts.

54. (Below) *The Hat Battery*, as illustrated in George Dodd's *Days at the Factories* (1843), is a water-filled kettle heated from below by a coal fire. Several hatters work around it simultaneously; they are wetting, rolling, pressing, and blocking the hat bodies. Courtesy Merrimack Valley Textile Museum, North Andover, Massachusetts.

table or bench in a small, closetlike room (to keep the fiber in a confined space), with the bow hung from the ceiling [53]. When struck, the bow's vibrations loosened and spread the fur into a rounded triangular or oval batt. The batt was covered by wet linen or paper and pressed and kneaded gently by hand until a minimum of hardening was achieved.

A hollow, conical cap (variously called a "hood," "cone," or "body") was next formed by joining two batts together: the first batt, now hardened, was covered by a triangular-shaped cloth or paper liner, smaller on all sides than the batt itself. The uncovered edges of the batt were folded over on top of the liner. A second batt was then placed over this, with its edges folded over or wrapped around the edges of the first. Through continued working and pressure, the batts were joined together, forming a body. This was in turn moistened, rolled, and rerolled until it was strong enough for fulling.

The fulling bath was usually in a trough or battery with sides of sloping wooden planks [54]. Besides boiling water, some form of acid, wine lees, or tartar might be included in the bath. The body was boiled for as many as seven hours and then repeatedly rolled and worked over the planks, periodically being dipped in the boiling water. When necessary, more fur was added to the weak spots. By the time this *planking* had been completed, the body had shrunk by about one half. In some cases, the nap was also roughed up after planking with a horsehair cloth.

Up until this time, the body was still a basic conical shape. It was next shaped into a hat [55]. The bottom edge was worked—turned up and pushed down in such a way as to first form a ringlike fold and then several concentric folds. The body was moistened, put over a wooden mold, and worked further, usually with a stick, until the center was stretched and smooth. By the end of this process, a distinct part hung down below the mold; this was later turned up to form the brim. The surface of the hat was also finished while on the mold: it was either rubbed or shorn to make a smooth surface, or brushed with a carder to bring up the nap.

Most hats were dyed black. The hat was alternately immersed in a dyebath (primarily of logwood, galls, or oak bark), and allowed to dry in the air, about eight times in all. A dressing or stiffening solution usually followed. This was originally made of vinegar and some other material—ox bile or a concoction of horse-chestnut leaves and glue, for example—but from the beginning of the 19th century mixtures of shellac, turpentine, tartar, and mastic were used. Hats were often made *extremely* stiff—in 1824, McClellan tells us, top hats made in Pennsylvania were stiff enough to support a 200-pound man! Some were also waterproofed with materials such as resin, beeswax, mutton, and suet; the exact formulas were highly prized secrets.

Other finishing procedures included trimming the brim and brushing, steaming, and ironing. The last was done with a "hatter's goose," an iron heated by a red-hot slug placed in its hollow core [56]. Most hats were then lined and later fitted with leather sweat bands on the inside and hatbands on the outside.

55. In this 16th-century woodcut of a hatter and his apprentices, a number of hat styles are visible. The man at the left may be beating the hat body with a stick; the boy seated in the center is trimming the brim.

56. A "hatter's goose" or iron, after an illustration in John Thomson's 1868 treatise on hatmaking. The back opens so a hot slug can be inserted. Illustration Jeanne Freer.

CHAPTER THREE

Commercial Felt and Feltmaking

The first mechanical process for the production of wool felt was invented by an American, J.R. Williams, in about 1820. A few years later felt production began in earnest when Robert Bacon of Winchester, Massachusetts, started manufacturing hats and slippers. Several mills were opened after the Civil War and, by 1900, there were 12 in all. Manufactured felt was used for a variety of clothing items: overcoats, skirts, hats, leggings, gaiters, mittens, and linings. Coverings for steam cylinders and boilers, linings for "watertight" ships, and polishing cushions for jewelers and marble cutters were also made.

Maturin Murray Ballou, author of *The Pictorial Drawing Room Companion*, described the feltmaking process he saw in the Union Manufacturing Company in Norwalk, Connecticut, in 1855:

> Sixteen layers of cross-lapped wool batts are drawn over a table, a section of which is covered with a perforated plate lying upon a steam box, through which, as it is two minutes passing, the wool becomes thoroughly enlivened by the hot vapor. It then passes under a platten [platen] of great weight and motion.

Other early hardening machines consisted of sets of wooden rollers heated from below. The wool batts were arranged between two pieces of cloth and fed through the vibrating rollers.

After the turn of the century, more mills were opened. Heavy felt overcoats, cloaks, and capes were popular at this time, as were felt petticoats. Saddlery felts—the whole range of horse trappings, including blankets, saddle cloths, collar pads, and a variety of trimmings—were important, too. Felt was also used by plumbers in the early part of the century for water tap washers and pipe covers, and by builders as insulation for foundations and roofs.

ROLL FELT

Today's standard roll or pressed felt is made as continuous fabric yardage—up to 50 or 60 yards long and 56 to 80 inches wide. (The name comes from the fact that the felt rolls off the presses and is wound onto rolls.) This is the kind of felt most people are familiar with, for the common dime-store novelty felt is made this way. While the qualities of roll felt can vary a great deal, it tends to be relatively thin—no thicker than one inch—and soft and pliable.

The processes involved in making wool roll felt are essentially extensions of the earlier methods. The wool is first sorted as to type, grade, color, and so forth and unusable parts of the fleece removed. It is then scoured in a series of tanks filled with successively weaker alkali solutions, dried, and *carbonized* if necessary. Carbonizing is a method of removing vegetable matter from wool by applying a weak sulfuric-acid solution, thus destroying the cellulose but leaving the wool unaffected. Heat then turns the decomposed material to carbon, which is crushed to a fine powder and vacuumed out.

Fibers can be blended at this point. Virgin wool may be combined with wool noils (short fibers that were removed from wool spun into yarn), wool wastes (short fibers thrown off in the machines during carding and spinning), or garnetted wool (fibers reclaimed from yarn or cloth that was thoroughly torn apart). Cotton, rayon, and synthetic fibers may also be added, depending on the intended use of the felt. The various fibers are weighed out in specific proportions and blown together in a blending bin.

Carding—the process of opening up snags, loosening the fibers, and arranging them in a parallel manner—is done on rotating cylinders covered with fine wire teeth [57]. The wool comes off the rollers as a very thin, wide (nearly 8 feet) web, which is rolled onto an apron via a circular conveyor belt. Two sets of carding machines, set at right angles to one another, feed alternately onto the same apron. In this way a batt of perpendicular layers is built up, with an equal number of fibers in both the crosswise and lengthwise directions. The thickness may vary considerably; between 4 and 20 layers might be used.

Hardening, the next step, may also take place on an endless canvas apron. The apron moves forward in sections, with each section successively undergoing the same operations. The batt is brought to a steam table and thoroughly saturated, then compressed between two steel platens (about 100 pounds per square foot) and subjected to intense vibration [58]. The pressure, the continual vibration, and the heat and moisture cause the fibers to felt together. When one section of the batt has been hardened long enough, the top platen rises automatically and the apron moves forward, bringing another section into position. Many batts are often hardened simultaneously, meshing together into one thick piece of felt. This process is called the flat or plate hardening method.

Some felts, particularly those to be used for cushioning and padding, are ready for use after hardening. Most industrial felts, however, require a fair degree of strength and firmness and these are always milled or fulled. Fulling can be quite dramatic; the felt may shrink as much as 50 percent. Although commercial feltmakers do not generally add soap or other lubricating agents in the hardening process, they do add them here. The hardest all-wool felts are treated with dilute sulfuric acid, but other felts, particularly those with vegetable fibers in them, may be treated with alkaline materials such as palm-oil soap.

Until recently (the last 25 to 30 years), all commercial fulling was done in fulling stocks or hammer mills—machines consisting of large bowls or bins in which huge, heavy hammers are driven by a crankshaft. The hardened felt is folded into the bowl and the hammers continually pound it, causing it to rotate slowly in

57. A commercial carding machine in a woolen mill. The sorted wool fiber is fed into the machine at the lower right, and is drawn through the series of rollers with fine wire teeth. The carded batt is fed off the machine on the other side, not visible in this photograph. Courtesy American Felt and Filter Company, Newburgh, New York.

the bowl as it is compressed and released [59]. Fulling might last anywhere from 5 minutes to 12 hours. Generally, fulling of this type causes little shrinkage in the width of the fabric.

Hammer mills are still in use in many places, but there are also rotary milling machines in which the material is stretched and compressed, causing less shrinkage in length. The felt moves through a series of rollers at extremely high speed. Some milling machines move both backward and forward, causing even greater compression.

The felt is thoroughly washed and treated to remove any resins, detergents, or acids. Natural-finish felt is dried and ready to use. Other felts are dyed, dried, and finished in various ways [60]. Dyeing is somewhat complex, for the nature of industrial felt fabric presents several problems. Its tight structure makes thorough dye penetration difficult and, where different fibers are combined, each will take the dye in a different way. In addition, the relative lack of surface texture in commercial felt means that color variation is highly visible. To overcome these problems, three to six dyestuffs are generally combined for a single color. When the felt is made from a combination of wool and cellulosic or synthetic fibers, furthermore, dyeing is often done in two steps: acid dyeing for the wool after neutralizing, direct dyeing for the other fibers.

After dyeing, the felt is placed in a centrifugal extractor or passed through mangle-type rollers to remove a good percentage of moisture. It may then undergo a variety of finishing treatments: stiffening (agents include potato, wheat, corn, or rice starch, or glue); softening; shrink and crease resistance (usually by means of a synthetic resin); impregnation with wax emulsions or graphite compounds for water repellency; mothproofing; treatments to ward off microbiological attack; flame retardancy;

and rubberizing. After finishing, the felt is stretched out flat on tenterframes (stretching helps restore it to its original width) and dried with circulating hot air.

Final surface treatments are an integral part of commercial feltmaking. Soft and medium-hard felts are fed onto shearing machines where rapidly moving knives remove all surface fibers, leaving a smooth finish. Harder felts are usually sanded on drum sanding machines similar to those used in woodworking. Burling, or hand removal of surface impurities, and a *decatizing* process may follow. (Decatizing, a kind of shrinkproofing, consists of subjecting the felt to successive hot-steam and cold-air treatments.) Finally, it is pressed in cylindrical or vertical hydraulic presses.

SHEET FELT

Unlike roll felt, sheet or formed felt is made in fairly small pieces, typically 36 inches square. Also in contrast to roll felt, the sheets can be quite dense and thick (3 to 4 inches). There are also wheel felts—round pieces made from circular batts. Most wheel felts and a good percentage of sheet felts are made of 100-percent wool. These are the felts used for polishing and most wicking operations, as well as gaskets and other stamped or shaped pieces.

The manufacture of formed felt is essentially the same process already described above, but some of the steps require more manual labor. In preparing the batt for a felt wheel, for example, the carded webs are built up in perpendicular layers by hand. Each sheet or wheel is then hardened individually in a plate hardener. After fulling, this dense felt is so hard it can be shaped by being turned on a lathe [61]. Pieces of sheet felt can also be formed in a kind of extruding operation; some wicks, for example, may be forced through a die, shaped, and cut. Stiffening, softening, mothproofing, and water-repellency treatments are not generally necessary for sheet felt, but resins may be added to a polishing wheel that will undergo a great deal of abrasion. Sheet and wheel felts are never dyed.

HATS

Hatmaking machinery was introduced about the middle of the 19th century and, as hats became readily available, they were more popular than ever. With mechanization, the slow tedious process of hand bowing was no longer necessary and hats could also be shaped more quickly, efficiently, and consistently. Some operations were never successfully mechanized, however, and are still done by hand today.

Some beaver and wool hats are still made in hat factories, but rabbit is by far the most commonly used hat fiber. Many Stetson-type cowboy hats and businessman's dress hats, for example, are made of rabbit. Skins are imported from France and other countries where rabbit meat is popular, and they are used in great quantities—as many as 14 skins in one hat. The skins are soaked in water until they soften and expand and the fur is removed and carrotted in a solution of nitric acid and hydrogen peroxide. When dry, it goes through a blower that helps loosen the fiber and remove the dirt. The heavier and longer hair fibers separate from the short fur fibers automatically during the blowing by falling to the floor.

60. Long rolls of felt are washed, dyed, and often finished with sizes and other treatments. Here it is being dyed. Courtesy Merrimack Valley Textile Museum, North Andover, Massachusetts.

61. Wool sheet felts are turned on a lathe, much as wood might be. Here felt is being trimmed to form "rock hard" buffing wheels like those at bottom. Courtesy Merrimack Valley Textile Museum, North Andover, Massachusetts.

The fur is sucked into a cylindrical chamber outfitted with a large, slowly rotating cone made of stainless steel or copper mesh. Cones come in a variety of sizes, each about five times the size of the finished hat that will be made from it. Strong air currents under the cone attract the fur to the outside surface of the cone, where it settles into a thin web [62]. The blower and the cone chamber, then, effectively replace the hand operations of bowing and joining together two triangular batts.

In some factories, another slightly larger cone is placed over the fur-covered one. In all plants, the cone is then covered with damp burlap and submerged in a vat of hot water and acetic acid, a mixture that helps activate the carrotting chemicals and start the felting process. When the hat body is slightly hardened and removed from the metal cone, it is worked by hand—folded, rolled, and kneaded with a circular motion so shrinkage will be equal on all sides. From time to time it is opened to ensure that the sides don't stick together. This is an amazing process to watch; the workers are so skilled it is hard to see what they are doing with their rapid motions. The felt is wetted down in hot water and worked continually, either by hand or by a machine consisting of a series of drums or rollers. The hat bodies are rolled in flannel and manually fed into it, one at a time. By the time the rolling is complete, the body becomes irreversibly felted and has shrunk to the proper hat size.

Dyeing usually takes place at this point. Hat bodies are turned inside out, fluffed up, and fed into a chamber, about 12 dozen at a time. They are tumbled with the dye for about three hours [63].

The first part of shaping and blocking is done on a machine with metal fingers that work the felt both at the top, or crown, and at the brim. Alternate hot- and cold-water baths help set the shape. A shaping machine in use about 40 years ago worked on a very interesting principle: the body was placed crown downward in a hollow metal form and a heavy rubber balloon placed inside it. The mold was covered and steamed and the balloon filled with water until it completely filled the body. Pressure from both inside and outside, coupled with the steam, had the effect of ironing the hat as it was shaped.

Hat brims are treated with shellac today much as they were in

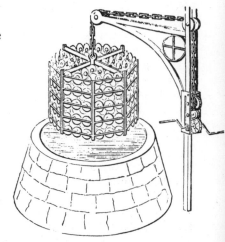

63. A 19th-century "cage and cauldron" for dyeing hats. New dyeing chambers operate on the same principle.

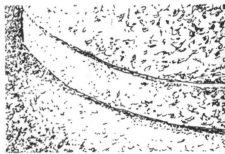

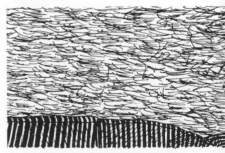

64. In this 19th-century hat factory, workers shape the hats on rotating wooden blocks.

the 19th century. The hat is placed on a special block and, when a lever is pushed, shellac is automatically released—enough to permeate the brim but not the body of the hat.

Final blocking is done on poplar molds specially made for particular hat styles and sizes. All hats are then sanded as they revolve on a lathelike machine. In some cases, special, luxurious finishes are aimed for. "Velour" hats, for example, are made from particularly long fur that is brushed up and clipped after blocking to make a soft, pilelike surface; hats with a "sponge" or "pebble" finish have a nubby surface created by knobs of fur [65]. Brims are cut, edges rounded, and leather hat bands and linings are then added to most commercial hats [66].

Wool felt hats are usually made largely from noils, the short fine fibers grown next to the skin of the sheep. The first steps in their manufacture are a little different from those already described. The wool is carded and the loose web of fiber is automatically wrapped continuously around a metal cone, forming a body about an inch thick and a foot and a half high. Later, hardened wool felt hats may also go through a fulling mill, where they are treated like any sheet felt.

The demand for felt hats declined dramatically from the end of World War II through the 1960s, as men chose to go bareheaded for the first time in centuries. Although the production of fur-felt hats is now leveling off, there is a significant increase in wool-felt hat production. Interestingly, cowboy-style hats are among those most in demand today.

65. Two modern hat finishes: rough and pitted "pebble" finish (top) and a smooth "silk" finish (above). Illustration Jeanne Freer.

66. The "press room" of a 19th-century New England hat factory.

COMMERCIAL FELT TODAY

The felt industry has undergone a great many changes since the Second World War. The most striking one is the relative decline in the production of pure wool felt. With the extensive development of manmade and synthetic fibers, coupled with the rising price of wool, roll felt is made with an increasingly larger percentage of synthetic fibers. Meanwhile, needled felts made entirely of synthetic fibers are becoming more and more common.

Industry decides whether to use all-wool, wool-blend, or all-synthetic felt based solely on practical considerations. The commercial world uses felt as an engineering material whose properties can be varied for particular purposes, much as plastic or metal can be. Most felt manufactured today is "technical" felt, made to specification for each product and use. The feltmaker's major concerns, therefore, are with density and hardness, surface quality and treatment, and shape or form. Even small differences in the felt can make tremendous differences in the felt products. In wicking operations, for example, a dense felt might allow 6 drops of a fluid to flow through each minute, while slightly more porous felt would allow up to 10 drops a minute.

Different fibers are blended together to produce hybrid felts with special characteristics. Cotton mixed with wool, for example, will decrease the density of the material, a property useful in filtering; or nylon might be added to increase the tensile strength and abrasive properties of wool. Kapok, a vegetable fiber, increases felt's ability to absorb sound and its insulating properties. On the other hand, all-wool felt might be chosen if it is to be used in an acidic environment. Synthetic fibers deteriorate far more readily in such an atmosphere, though they stand up better than wool in alkaline conditions. If felt will be used to filter liquid with a high vinegar content, such as pickles, then wool might be best. Synthetic felt might be better, however, if a filter is needed to remove deposits from hard, calcium-laden (alkaline) water. Wool is also better than synthetic fiber where high heat is generated, for it has a higher melting point and is far less flammable. Synthetic fibers stand up better in abrasive applications.

All these factors must be balanced against one another. For example, a resin-treated wool felt would generally be used in a polishing operation, for although it might wear down more quickly than a synthetic needled felt, it would better withstand the heat generated by constant abrasion.

Many items traditionally made of felt are now being made of other materials, most notably foams and plastics. But as Niran Bates Pope, a representative of the felt industry, put it in *Everybody Uses Felt* (1950):

> It is a significant comment on the unique character of felt that for every productive line that has expired by natural limitations, a new field of demand has appeared. Thus the advent of the automobile and agricultural implement industries almost entirely eliminated animal traction and saddlery felts over the years, [but they] created a huge demand for felt and caused the industry to expand.

So, while felt insulation formerly used in airplanes is superseded by other materials, felt linings find a new application in Gemini spacesuits for astronauts [67].

Felt is also now being impregnated with, laminated to, or combined with other materials so the properties of both can be exploited. Nonskid felt-laminate bases are used, for example, as cushions under small vibrating equipment such as electric fans, sewing machines, and typewriters. An electric clothes dryer uses a polyester fiber felt impregnated with silicone rubber as a seal on the exhaust end of the dryer drum. In trains, a synthetic sponge-rubber pad is covered by a felt wick and used as a journal lubricator (the journal is the part of the axle that turns in a bearing). The sponge holds the excess oil, the felt controls its flow and absorbs vibration [68].

Familiarity with the wide range of commercial applications for felt should provide a clearer understanding of the adaptability, characteristics, and possibilities of the material and serve as inspiration for the creative use of handmade felt.

67. Felt was used as an insulating layer just beneath the surface layer of the Gemini EVA Suit. Courtesy National Aeronautics and Space Administration.

68. A sponge rubber and felt journal lubricator is about to be slipped into position underneath the journal of a freight car. Photo, originally taken by the United States Rubber Company in the 1940s, courtesy Merrimack Valley Textile Museum, North Andover, Massachusetts.

CHAPTER FOUR

Basic Feltmaking

It is just in the last few years that artists have begun to seriously explore the feltmaking process and the almost unlimited artistic possibilities of handmade felt. Curiously, this exploration occurs at a time when the world production of true felt is declining rapidly. More and more of the world's nomads are settling in permanent locations, many Central Asians are replacing felt-covered yurts with other types of shelter. At the same time, clothing traditionally made of felt is being replaced by more "modern" fabrics. In the Western world, hats are no longer *de rigeur* for either men or women—they have almost become a novelty item—and felt is but rarely used for garments such as coats and skirts. Industry is using less and less wool in its felt, more often than not turning to synthetic needled felts and chemically bonded, non-woven fabrics.

Happily, the artist is less concerned with market conditions or the most up-to-date products and styles. He or she may use traditional materials and techniques, turning them to artistic ends. As an artistic process, felting is very adaptable and satisfying.

WHY MAKE FELT

Perhaps the most basically satisfying aspect of feltmaking is its directness and simplicity. The inherent characteristics of the material—wool—are not changed in the process. On the contrary, they are beautifully revealed. Given the right conditions, it is in the very nature of wool to felt: there is a minimum amount of technique and equipment to hinder creativity; there is nothing to get between the feltmaker and the felt. Felting is physically involving as well, as many artists have commented on:

Deborah Kaufman: "I like the physical involvement in working on a large piece, using my whole body strength to knead it, then feeling physically tired when the piece is complete."

Cheryl Patton McManamy: "I came to felting at a time when I needed to exert energy almost violently. Felting was the release I found."

Diane Brawarsky: "An intimacy develops between me and the piece as I pound and knead the fibers, feeling the felt forming. The process is an integral part of the piece."

Georgia Stegmeier: "[Seeing] the transformations that take place in each step . . . brings me close to the material."

The quality of handmade felt that stands out above all others is its rich, tactile, and textural surface, its primal wooliness. "Wool to me means warmth, insulation, and protection," remarks Diane Lomen, "and felting is a superb [technique] to bring out these qualities." "Its density, warmth, and thickness invite touch, draw me closer, and make me want to wrap up in it," admits Patricia Townsend. As Susan Marie Cunningham explains, "it's hard to talk about felt without touching it." Beth Beede also likes the warm feel of it as well as its smell, while Marleah Drexler MacDougal loves its earthy texture.

"The ambiguities, the irregularities, the subtleties, the contradictions" of handmade felt appeal to Ruth Geneslaw. And contradictions there are. The surface can be rough, pitted, and bumpy or it can be smooth, almost silky. It can even look hard and soft at the same time. Some artists call it a "painterly" medium and prefer to work with images on the surface. Others call it sculptural and "deal with the whole body of the material," as Beth Beede puts it.

Felt is also remarkably versatile. It can be made in any size or shape and, as Barbara Setsu Pickett points out, there are no "line-forming planes" as there are in weaving. Even the lack of a feltmaking tradition in the West can prove liberating to feltmakers. Laura Basanta remarks that the object made of felt "is not tied to past boundaries."

Felt can be cut or torn in any direction, molded, shaped, and even carved. By its very nature it entraps other things in itself, but it can also be trapped or stuffed into something else. It can act as a fabric, with all the draping, mobile qualities that implies, or it can be a firm, immobile background. As a surface it can also be printed on, painted, or embossed. It can be cut into elements for a linear construction; combined with weaving, crochet, embroidery, or any other technique; it may even act as a bridge between diverse techniques and media. Felt also presents innumerable possibilities for color exploration.

Finally, results are very immediate in feltmaking: a small piece of plain felt can generally be made in less than an hour. Compared to most other craft techniques, particularly fiber techniques, this is quite fast. It is exciting and gratifying to work on something that yields such quick results.

Lynn Sullivan speaks for many artists who have been struck by and delighted with this unusually versatile medium: "Once I began, the potential of the technique expanded faster than I could keep up with it."

MATERIALS FOR FELTMAKING

Wool is the main ingredient of handmade felt. Any kind of wool will felt, but the ease with which it hardens and the quality of the felt will vary considerably with different wools. Some of today's feltmakers like to work with long-staple wool, particularly the long lustrous fleece from Australia. Scientific research indicates, however, that a short to medium wool is usually the easiest to work with. Very long fibers are likely to be coarse and have a relatively wide crimp. They often mat together without truly felting and produce a thick spongy felt in which individual fibers are clearly visible. Very short fibers, even those taken from a new lamb, will felt well but are difficult to control. They felt very quickly and produce an extremely solid, hard felt with an even, compact surface. Felt made from fine, short wool also tends to shrink more than felt made from coarser, longer wool. (It should be understood that these are generalities. There are actually a great many factors that affect the felting qualities of a particular wool: how the sheep was raised, when it was shorn, and so forth.)

In the felt industry, the preferred wool staple length is about 1½ to 2 inches. This corresponds roughly to the so-called medium-wooled sheep breeds. Hampshire, Suffolk, Dorset, and Southdown sheep, for example, have an average yearly staple of 2 to 2½ inches. Cheviot, Oxford, and Shropshire sheep have a somewhat longer staple—on average about 3 inches—but they are still considered medium-wooled sheep. Fine-wool breeds such as Merino and Rambouillet have a staple of approximately 2½ inches, but they are very soft, with a narrow (compact) crimp [69]. They felt well, but because they are expensive and in great demand for spinning, are probably not the best choice for felt-making. A chart depicting the qualities of various breeds of sheep will be found in the Appendix.

69. These two photographs illustrate how widely variable the crimp on different fleece can be. Photo Larry Beede.

Ultimately, the type of wool you use will depend on what you can get and what works best for you. You may find a local sheep owner who is willing to give or sell you a fleece, or you may already have a bit of Merino or very long wool on hand. (Lynn Sullivan of Australia sometimes finds it difficult to get anything *but* Merino!) You may like working with the longer wool, or you may find your particular project simply works better with it. Experiment with different kinds of fleece to discover what pleases you most.

The wool need not be all new, virgin fleece. You can take a hint from industrial feltmakers, who often use wool noils (short, kinky wool fibers that are separated from the long staple in woolen and worsted spinning), card waste, and garnetted or reprocessed wools. All of these fibers are fluffed open and mixed together, recarded, and then felted along with top-quality wool. You might be able to get wool waste, noils, or reprocessed wool from local manufacturers. If not, you might find you can felt some of your own wool waste: failed pieces of felt, short pieces of fleece you picked out of your hand cards, trimmings from a handmade pile rug, and so on. In Scotland, felt was made from picked-over wool not considered good enough to be spun, so you will be following a tradition that is part of our Western heritage. For best results, mix this reused wool with at least 20 percent of new wool.

It is also possible to make felt from commercially prepared wool *roving* or *top* (long "ropes" of combed, unspun, or very lightly spun fiber). Use a fairly thick, soft roving and cut or break it into lengths somewhat longer than you want the finished felt to be. Open it up as much as you can to loosen the fibers and be sure to overlap the pieces carefully when preparing the batt. Essentially, you will be using the pieces of roving as if they were carded rolags (rolls prepared on hand cards) or batts.

For your first felting experiments I suggest you use pure wool. You will become comfortable with the process and develop a sensitivity to the steps involved without adding any new and confusing variables. Once confident you know how to make felt, though, feel free to experiment with other materials. You can work almost any other fiber in with wool: doghair, alpaca, cotton, silk, kapok, flax, jute, polyester, Mylar, rayon, feathers, or whatever. You can be as inventive as you wish. Save the hair and fur you brush from your cat or dog—or for that matter save the hair you pull out of your own hairbrush. Try using cotton balls (the kind sold in drugstores) or polyester fiberfill sold by the bag for stuffing. Gather the fibers from milkweed pods or burst-open cattails in the fall. Work in pieces of steel wool or loofa sponge, or use the down from an old, leaky feather pillow. I was even able to work the shredded fibers my mother raked out of a new nylon shag carpet into some of my felt.

In trying to determine how much of these other fibers to use, remember it is the wool that will be doing the actual felting; the other fibers are merely acting as filler. If you want a strong felt, use as much wool as possible. If you are primarily concerned with texture and don't care too much about strength, you can add quite a bit of other material. In general, you should not use less than 25 or 30 percent wool. Also keep in mind that if you are using a sizable proportion of other fibers, you are best off using high-quality, virgin wool. Reprocessed wool or wool noils would in this case be too short and weak to surround and bind the filler properly.

You may well be wondering if felt can be made solely with other fibers—with no wool at all. The answer is yes. You can felt many other materials, but the quality of the felt will vary considerably. Most animal-hair fibers will form some kind of felt; fibers closest to sheep's wool will of course felt best. Mohair (from the angora goat), with its relatively long coarse fibers, will tend to felt like a long-staple wool. Alpaca usually forms a very dense, hard felt, which shrinks a great deal in the process and does not have the buoyancy of wool felt. Llama is probably similar, but I have never tried using it. Camel hair, made up largely of very soft, short fibers, tends to make a thin, fuzzy, soft felt that is hard to control and keep even throughout; holes were a constant problem in my experiments. Camels, like dogs, cats, goats, and other animals, actually have two kinds of hair—long, straight "guard" hairs (usually found on the back) and shorter, softer undercoat hairs (often called fur, found on the underside or stomach area). These different fibers felt very differently and are often separated (as in the industrial blowing machine that separates rabbit hair and rabbit fur). Combinations of both the short and long hairs from camel, dog, and other animals may work best for hand feltmakers, who usually cannot or do not want to undertake carrotting or chemical pretreatment of the short fur fibers.

Short stiff fibers are difficult to work with, but *can* be successfully felted. Cowhair is routinely used commercially for felt rug liners. Debra Rappaport uses the rough hard fiber sold for upholstery stuffing (it is commercially referred to as horsehair, but she claims it's actually a blend of hog and cowhair) in some of her large felt pieces. Human hair has been felted, too: felt from the straight hair of Chinese people was recently used in a New Hampshire factory for polishing glass—*after* it had been used for straining impurities out of peanut butter!

Vegetable fibers by themselves are not technically capable of felting, but as I explained in Chapter One, they can be beaten and made to stick together. In "The Early History of Felt," Laufer quotes a man who testified in 1845 before the Academy of Inscriptions and Letters of Paris:

> I have macerated unbleached flax in vinegar saturated with salt, and after compression have obtained a felt, with a power of resistance quite comparable with that of the famous armor of Conrad of Montferrat; seeing that neither the point of a sword, nor even balls discharged from fire-arms were able to penetrate it.

This "felt" is probably a form of paper, but its strength comes from the interlacing and interlocking of the strong flax fibers.

PREPARING THE MATERIALS

The fibers must first be loosened and separated from foreign debris such as burrs and sticks. They may or may not be cleaned; some people feel strongly that washing is advantageous, others that it is not. When unwashed wool is used, the hardening process may take longer and it may be difficult to make a very strong felt. Unwashed fleece is more slippery than washed fleece, and the fibers have a tendency to slide past one another rather than interlock. Furthermore, the hot-water-and-soap solution you apply to the felt batt will first have to clean the fleece—it is not until most of the dirt and lanolin are out that true felting begins. On the other hand, more control may be possible with unwashed fleece, precisely because it does take longer to felt. Some feltmakers believe they get a softer, richer felt with greasy wool. Other people simply do not want to take the time to wash the wool first and find the results of felting with unwashed wool perfectly adequate.

When you *do* wash your wool, there are just a few general rules to keep in mind: essentially, you don't want to subject the wool to conditions that will tend to make it felt—not at this stage. It should not go through extremes in temperature or through severe agitation or pressure. Don't put it under a faucet of running water, don't wring it out, don't boil or freeze it. Lay it gently in an already filled basin of water. Use a gentle soap like Ivory, rather than a harsh detergent. Fleece becomes surprisingly clean after soaking in soapy water just a few minutes [Step 1]. Lynda Lowe Oren recommends soaking wool in sudsy ammonia (one cup to a gallon of water) instead of soap. Ammonia, like soap, dissolves the lanolin and pulls the dirt out of the fiber.

The wool must be dry in order to be carded [Step 2]. It will dry much more quickly if hung in a vertical position, for the water actually rolls off the fiber. If you cannot hang it vertically or you are unconcerned with the length of time it takes to dry, spread it out on a screen, cheesecloth, plastic mesh, or some other surface that allows air to circulate on all sides. (If you use window screening, be sure it is aluminum; metal will rust and contaminate the wool with iron.) If necessary, it can also be speed-dried with an electric fan or hairdryer.

When dry, the wool should be gently pulled or picked apart ("teased") to loosen the fibers [Step 3]. Next, arrange it on hand cards or a drum carding machine and card until straight and smooth [Steps 4–9]. The finished rolags (from the hand cards) or batts (from the drum carder) will then be ready for the felt batt.

Some handspinners feel they do not have the same control over the fleece with a carding machine that they have with hand cards; handmade rolags are usually finer and more even than machine-made batts. For felting purposes, however, the batts are completely adequate (if not superior) and the increased speed makes the carding machine a real blessing.

Perhaps the easiest way to make felt is to use commercially prepared wool batts. Some woolen mills will card fleece you send them into long batts, and/or sell batts made up from their own wool. These are sold primarily for use as quilt filler, and come in thick, bedsize sheets. Pieces can be peeled or torn off and treated like drum-carded batts. I have found these a real delight to use, for they felt easily, quickly, and evenly. They do produce a very white felt—a little too white for some effects—because they are made from bleached wool, but they can be dyed or "antiqued" (see Chapter Six).

It *is* possible to make felt with uncarded wool, but it will probably not be smooth or even. In carding, the wool fibers are stretched out, separated from one another, and distributed evenly throughout the rolag or batt. This means there will be roughly the same amount of fiber in each section of the felt batt and the density of the hardened felt will remain consistent. If you use

Step 1: Washing. To wash the wool, fill a basin, tub, or large pot with lukewarm water and dissolve Ivory Flakes or another mild soap in it. Gently submerge the wool, covering it completely with water, and let it soak 10 to 15 minutes. Lift the wool out and put it aside while you pour out the dirty water. Refill the basin with fresh, lukewarm water. If you think the wool can be cleaned further, add soap to this fresh water and soak for an hour or more. If it seems clean, use clear water for rinsing. Resubmerge the wool. Continue lifting it out and putting it in baths of clear water of about the same temperature until all soap and dirt are removed. Photo Larry Beede.

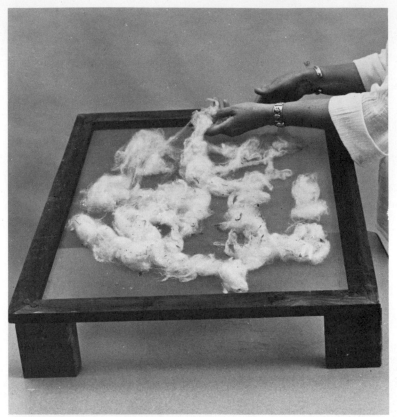

Step 2: Drying. If possible, dry the clean wool by hanging it in a vertical position—perhaps draping it over a tree branch or a clothesline. It can also be dried on an aluminum or plastic screen that allows air to circulate freely around it. Spread the wool out as much as possible in a single thin layer. Photo Larry Beede.

Step 3: Teasing. Tease (pick) the wool by pulling it apart lightly but firmly until you have a soft, fluffy mass of fiber. Loose dirt not removed by washing should fall out in this process. Photo Larry Beede.

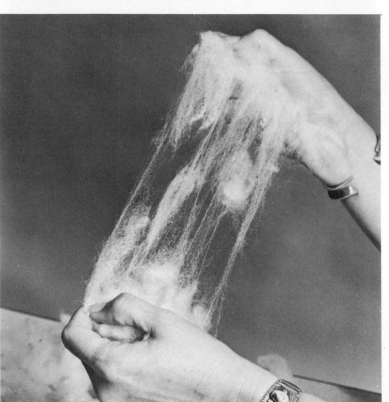

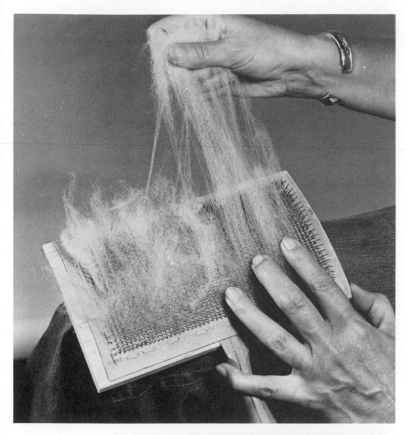

Step 4: Hand Carding. When using hand cards to prepare the wool, sit comfortably on a chair with your legs slightly apart. Rest the left-hand card on your knee and lay small pieces of teased wool on the card, stretching it out as you go. The fiber should catch in the teeth about half an inch from the top of the card; it can extend over the edge. Try to fill the card evenly with a thin layer of wool all the way across. Photo Larry Beede.

Step 5: Hand Carding. Take the right-hand card and draw it teeth-down across the left-hand card. Do this with enough pressure so the teeth glide through one another, but not enough so they get caught in one another. Repeat the motion several times. Most of the wool will by now be on the right-hand card. Photo Larry Beede.

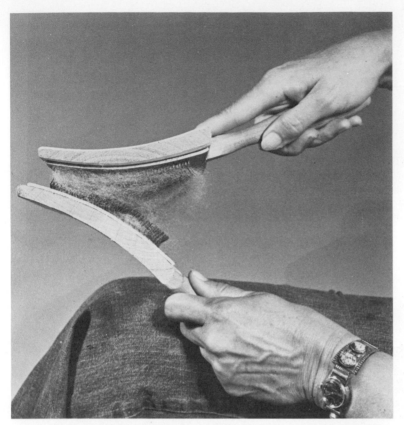

Step 6: Hand Carding. The wool must be transferred back to the left-hand card. Slowly draw the right-hand card toward you, moving firmly across the other. The wool should stay behind. Repeat Step 6 as many times as necessary to make the fleece completely smooth and parallel. Part of the fiber will be hanging from the bottom edge of the left-hand card. Photo Larry Beede.

Step 7: Hand Carding. (Left) Use the wooden edge or the back of the right-hand card to roll the fleece off the left-hand card. Work toward you, or in the direction of the handle. Push gently; use your fingers if necessary to tuck the roll in as you go. Photo Larry Beede.

Step 8: Drum Carding. If you are using a drum-type carding machine, feed the teased wool onto the tray as evenly as you can and begin to turn the crank. The wool will feed in automatically. Photo Larry Beede.

Step 9: Drum Carding. When all the wool is smoothly on the drums, find the point in the large drum where there is a break in the teeth. Insert a knitting needle or thin stick in this opening and gently lift the wool up off the teeth. Open the batt by cutting or tearing it where it has been lifted. Then turn the crank in reverse and roll the opened batt off the machine. Photo Larry Beede.

uncarded wool, some areas of the finished felt will probably be thicker than others and it will have less overall strength. Depending on what the felt is intended for, you may wish to explore the effects of working this way. Remember, the Tibetan nomads made felt from unloosened, uncarded fleece, which was relatively soft and smooth on one side and shaggy on the other.

All other materials you will be adding to the felt should be prepared in much the same way as the wool. They should be clean, loose and separate, and, if possible, combed. This means if you are adding cat or dog hair to the wool, it should be washed and picked apart, and possibly carded. Cotton balls or polyester fiberfill should be picked and teased by hand.

If you are trying to make a consistently blended fiber felt, mix the other fibers with the wool at the carding stage. This will ensure that all fibers are equally distributed. You might of course be seeking a different effect: perhaps contrasting fibers on the felt surface only, or a layer of different fiber sandwiched between layers of wool.

I do not know of anyone making handmade felt entirely from fur fibers. There is a great deal of room for exploration in this area, but appropriate methods of pretreating the fiber (homestyle carrotting, in effect) would have to be investigated.

LAYING THE BATT

The felt batt is made by layering rolls of carded wool on a backing material. Many materials are suitable for backing, as we have seen: Turkish feltmakers usually use a reed mat while Mongolian feltmakers use another piece of felt or a piece of leather. The Turks also use sackcloth or other types of grass mats. The Chinese use rugs made of thin bamboo and the Iranians sometimes use canvas. Any material that will keep the wool in place, allow soap and water through, and hold up to severe agitation and rolling will do.

One backing material I like very much is nylon mosquito netting, which is sold by the yard in camping-supply stores and some hardware stores. The netting is durable, inexpensive, and it works beautifully. Many people like to use an old sheet or a piece of muslin, but netting has an important advantage: water tends to run over and off the sides of woven cloth, which often pushes the wool toward the edges of the batt. Water goes right through the mosquito netting, on the other hand, and saturates the wool evenly and thoroughly. The batt stays in place. It is also much easier to watch the felt's progress when it's inside netting.

Barbara Setsu Pickett and Lynda Lowe Oren recommend fiberglass screening as a backing material, which has many of the same advantages as mosquito netting. I have also tried using cheesecloth, reasoning that it is a net of sorts, too. Cheesecloth works, but the little cotton fibers felt in with the wool to some degree and can be almost impossible to remove. Nylon net (the kind bridal veiling is now made of) is usually not strong enough to hold up to the agitation of feltmaking. Solid woven fabrics other than cotton are also satisfactory: polyester, nylon, and other synthetic fabrics are fine, as long as they are not so smooth and slippery as to be difficult to work with. Bamboo matchstick shades also work beautifully with one particular felting method, which will be discussed below.

The batt must be prepared carefully, for it is literally the foundation of the felt. In order to prevent holes, the rolags or batts should be arranged so they slightly overlap one another within each layer; the different layers must also be placed at right angles to one another, or cross lapped [Step 10]. Cross lapping is the basis of a felt that is strong enough to take continued pressure in any direction. In Ballou's description of a visit to the Union Manufacturing Company in Norwalk, Connecticut, in 1855, he points out what used to happen when the layers of wool were not cross lapped:

> It was soon found that . . . there was nothing to blind it [to fill in holes] . . . and when it was made into garments, wherever it was stretched, as at the elbow of a coat, it left the mark of an indentation, there being no mechanical cohesion in its parts answering to the threads in ordinary fabrics, by which its original shape might be recovered.

Even in the felt industry today, the strongest felts are those where true perpendicular layering is done manually.

Spread the fiber as evenly as possible throughout the batt. If you are adding fibers other than wool and you have not carded them in, try to arrange them in a consistent fashion. Areas of the batt that are thicker than others will come out lumpy in the finished felt. Areas that are too thin may turn into holes.

Different fibers or wools can, of course, be purposely positioned for particular effects. When a fine wool is put on top of a coarse wool in one area only, for example, that area will felt more quickly and tend to pucker. A layer of commercially made felt, or one of poor, uneven, or hole-filled (failed) felt, can be

Step 10: Laying the Batt. Lay the rolags or batts next to one another on a piece of nylon mosquito netting. They should overlap slightly at the edges. Lay the second layer of rolags so it is 90°, or perpendicular, to the first layer. All subsequent layers should be put on in alternate directions: the third layer perpendicular to the second, and so on. Photo Larry Beede.

used as a base layer or interior layer in the wool batt. Here again, some puckering may result.

The number of layers comprising a batt will vary, of course, with the desired thickness of the felt. All batts must be at least two layers thick and, as a general rule, three layers are a good idea. Industrial feltmakers sometimes use as many as 16. Try using three or four layers in your first felting experiment. Later, try working with several more layers to produce a thick solid felt, then try only two layers to produce a thin felt.

If you have a specific project in mind for your finished felt, you will need to have an idea of how much the batt will shrink in the felting process. Unfortunately, it is difficult to know exactly; the amount of shrinkage in length, width, and depth depends on a combination of factors: the type of fleece or wool (and other materials, if any), the way the fleece was treated before felting (whether or not it was washed and with what kind of cleansing agent, how thoroughly it was carded, and so on), the temperature of the water, the type of hardening and fulling the batt was subjected to, and the length of time it was hardened.

I have felted commercially prepared, 10-inch batts of New Zealand wool in the washing machine and dryer and lost only about half an inch on each side—a shrinkage of about 10 percent. On the other hand, Hillary Farkas mentions a friend who made a large felted rug "by jumping on it every day for three weeks. She started out with a large, patio-size project and ended up with a piece she could roll under her arm."

In industry, where felt is hardened under a great deal of mechanical pressure, shrinkage can be up to 80 percent [70]. Felting wool by hand, you will generally find shrinkage to be between 15 and 45 percent [71]. (Other fibers, remember, shrink differently. Alpaca, for example, becomes extremely compact. Anne Dushanko-Dobek made a piece of alpaca-and-wool felt that shrank from 9 to 2¼ square feet.)

When you must have a reasonably good idea what the shrinkage of a particular felt will be, begin with one or more trial samples. Make a small piece of felt under the same conditions you would be using on the larger piece—the same fleece, water temperature, hardening action, and so on—and calculate the percentage it has shrunk. There are also a few rules of thumb to keep in mind: (1) fine wool shrinks more than coarse wool; (2) greasy, unwashed wool shrinks more than clean, washed wool; (3) increased hardening, which produces a denser felt, of course results in more shrinkage; (4) felt shrinks parallel to the direction it is moved during the hardening process. If you roll the felt repeatedly in one direction only, the fibers will orient and entangle themselves that way. The piece will shrink considerably in that direction and very little in the other.

SECURING THE BATT

In what I refer to as the basic felting method, the batt should be basted in place to prevent it from shifting during the hardening process [Steps 11–12]. Use a strong, heavy thread—dental floss is especially good—and long running stitches. You will actually be quilting, for the thread will be going through two pieces of fabric and a layer of stuffing. Many people find basting is only necessary along the edges of the wool, but for most control the stitching should cover the whole surface of the batt. Baste on the

70. "Thickness reduction and dimensional shrinkage attained in successive stages of felt manufacture," adapted from Pope's *Everybody Uses Felt*. This shows sectional views of different stages in commercial felt production. From bottom to top: initial raw stock, carded batt, hardened material, fulled material, finished felt.

71. The contrast between the felt batt (above) and finished, fulled felt (below) is not nearly as great when the felting is done entirely by hand as when it is done commercially. This felt is from drum-carded batts of long-staple New Zealand fleece, fulled with a rolling motion. Photo the author.

Step 11: Basting the Batt. Cover the layers of rolags—now a felt batt—with a second piece of nylon netting. Photo Larry Beede.

Step 12: Basting the Batt. Baste the batt to the two layers of netting with long quilting stitches. Be sure to secure the edges of the batt; stitch on the diagonal for the strongest hold. A sewing machine can be used for basting a relatively thin batt. Photo Larry Beede.

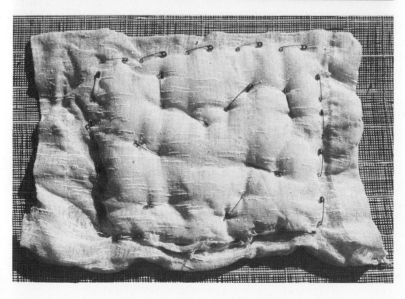

Alternate Step 12: Pinning the Batt. Long rustproof pins can be used in place of basting stitches when the batt is not too thick. Here, polyester curtain material is used as the backing fabric. Photo the author.

diagonal for the strongest hold and keep your stitches reasonably loose so they won't cause the batt to pucker.

A few feltmakers have tried to find less time-consuming methods of securing the batt to the backing fabric. Patricial Townsend experimented with long-reach staples. She was able to put the staples in very quickly, but found them difficult to remove after the felt was made. They also left slight indentations in the finished felt. These indentations might be put to use for interesting effects. Safety pins, inserted in the batt at frequent, regular intervals, can also be used instead of basting stitches [Alternate Step 12]. The pins don't leave the same kind of indentation and, because they are larger than staples, are not as difficult to remove. Be sure to use rustproof pins, but not diaper pins; their plastic tips may soften and melt, particularly if they are subjected to the intense heat of an electric dryer.

THE "BASIC" METHOD

Once the felt batt is prepared, it should be thoroughly saturated with hot water [Step 13]. Boiling water works well, but the hottest tap water will suffice. The heat and moisture make the wool fiber swell and expand, allowing each of its scales to open slightly. The felting process can begin. Since you cannot oversaturate the batt, feel free to use a great deal of water at this stage. The Khotans, a Mongolian nomadic people, use 40 to 50 liters (about 10½ to 13 gallons) of water for each roll of felt they make.

Although it is not completely necessary, it is helpful to add a lubricating or felting agent at this time. Generally, a mild alkaline agent is used. Industrial feltmakers often use a sulfuric-acid solution, however, which puzzled me for a long time, as acid can actually slow the felting process down. It is this very characteristic that is apparently exploited by commercial feltmakers, though, for they want an absolutely controlled product. The fibers on top and bottom of the batt are kept from felting too quickly, before the inside fibers have a chance to do so. A mild acid solution—or no lubricating agent at all—might be best, then, for a very thick felt. Under other circumstances, an alkaline agent is best. Most people I have questioned use soap, either in cake or liquid form. Soap gel is also convenient to use and easily stored. It can be made by dissolving about one cup of powdered or flaked soap in a gallon of water, and letting it sit for an hour or more. Detergent will also work well and sometimes seems to make the felting take place even more quickly than soap. Although some people claim detergent makes wool felt somewhat harsh, I have not noticed a significant difference in well-rinsed felt made with detergent or soap. Note that powdered detergent is probably better than liquid detergent in most cases. The latter contains a higher percentage of nonionic surfactants—ingredients that do not work in very hot (that is, boiling) water.

Wool felts more rapidly in soft water than in hard water. I suspect this is due to the fact that the soap solution lathers much more freely in soft water and thus does a better job as a lubricating agent. I don't notice any difference in the finished felt, but if your water is very hard, adding a water softener may mean less physical work for you, the feltmaker. Another consideration is possible damage to the felt from impurities in the water. For the chemicals that make water hard—principally calcium—and min-

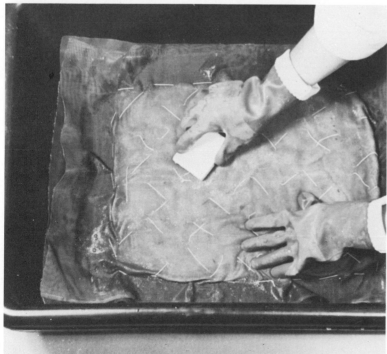

Step 13: Saturating the Batt. (Above) Put the quilted batt into a basin, tray, or sink and thoroughly saturate it with boiling (or very hot) water. A funnel attached to a watering-can spout (see inset) makes a good tool for dispensing hot water evenly on a large felt batt. Photo Larry Beede.

Step 14: Soaping and Hardening. (Left) Rub soap into the batt, using either a cake of soap or a solution made from liquid or powdered soap. Wear rubber gloves to protect your hands from the boiling water. Use the palms of your hands to press the felt, working from side to side and end to end. Photo Larry Beede.

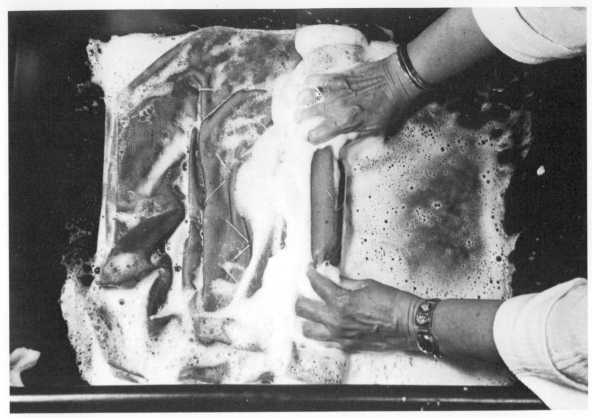

Step 15: Hardening. Continue working the batt with your hands, applying as much pressure as possible. Roll it tightly in one direction, kneading and pounding it; unroll and roll it in the other direction. Repeat this several times. It's helpful to establish a rhythm; you might sing a song or work to music with a regular beat. The rubber gloves can be removed when the water is no longer hot to the touch. Photo Larry Beede.

Step 15: Hardening and Fulling Alternatives. Different tools can be used to help agitate and apply pressure to the batt. Roll a rolling pin over the batt in all directions. Turn it over and work on the other side. Photo Larry Beede.

Step 15: Hardening and Fulling Alternatives. A paddle or mallet can be used to pound the batt, which may be either rolled or unrolled. Try pounding it both ways. Photo Larry Beede.

Step 15: Hardening and Fulling Alternatives. Work the batt against an old-fashioned washboard; again, work with it both rolled and unrolled. Photo Larry Beede.

erals such as iron can contaminate the wool during felting. To avoid eventual damage, use soft water that contains no calcium and less than .05 percent iron.

This brings us to the issue of whether or not to "shock" the wool by subjecting it to alternate baths of very hot and very cold water. Many of today's feltmakers do this, either here at the first stage of saturating and soaping the batt, or a little later, after the initial hardening. I feel there is no real reason to do this at all. Traditional feltmakers in Central Asia never used baths of different temperatures. One could argue that they did not have easy access to hot and cold water, but industrial feltmakers don't shock their felt either and they certainly could if they chose to. Shocking *is* done at the blocking stage in commercial hatteries (although when hats were made completely by hand, only boiling water was used) and in fulling already woven cloth, but in both these instances the concern is not with basic felting. It is the hot water that opens the fiber and allows it to felt; cold water only closes the fiber again.

The initial working of the felt is best done by hand, no matter how the rest of the hardening and fulling will proceed. The wet batt is still somewhat delicate and, if handled too roughly right away, may tear or come apart. The best way to begin hardening is to press the palms of your hands back and forth across the batt [Step 14]; follow this with rolling back and forth, first gently and later with more force [Step 15]. Any of the hardening and fulling procedures discussed below can be used [Step 15 Alternatives], as long as care is taken to ease into it; don't subject the batt to rough treatment before it has some dimensional stability.

An important thing to watch for, especially when felting for the first time, is the point at which the felt will hold together—the point when it has hardened. (This is also called the "soft felt" stage.) This may happen any time from 5 to 20 minutes after you begin to work the felt, depending on the kind of wool, felting agent, temperature, and amount and type of pressure/agitation you apply. The batt will begin to feel more like a whole unit and more responsive under your hands, much as bread dough does when kneaded to the point where the gluten holds it together. Pull on it gently to see if the wool will still move, or if it is locked in place. As Debra Glanz puts it, "it should no longer squish between your fingers." It should not stretch significantly in any direction with gentle pulling, but should still be capable of being manipulated with firm pulling. Put another way, you are looking for a solid, cohesive fabric you can shape, pull, and poke without having it come apart. Once the batt reaches this point, all further manipulation can be considered fulling.

When the felt is hardened, it is a good idea to remove the backing fabric and continue fulling with the batt uncovered [Step 16]. You will be better able to see what is happening and, if the backing might stick to the felt (as fiberglass screening or cheesecloth might), removing it now will minimize this. If the backing material is left on and the felt is worked until it becomes dense and hard, there may also be unwanted indentations left from the stitching or pins that held the material in place.

If there are any holes in the felt, it is possible to fill them in with more wool at this just-hardened stage. Carefully place carded wool in and around the hole and saturate it with a solu-

Step 16: Fulling. When the batt responds as a cohesive, solid unit and has hardened, you might choose to take it out of its backing fabric. Clip the basting stitches with a scissors. Photo Larry Beede.

tion of hot water and soap. Work it gently with your fingers—gently at first and later with more pressure—particularly at the edge of the hole where the felted and unfelted fibers overlap. When the patch has hardened to some extent, rework the whole batt with a good deal of pressure by rolling and rerolling, rubbing, or whatever. If the hole is particularly large, you may want to rewrap the batt in backing fabric for extra protection. The easiest way to do this is to use safety pins to secure the felt to the backing.

The shape of the batt can also be altered at this soft-felt stage. Pieces can be added and stuck together; thin edges can be folded in and thickened; and existing edges can be cut into new forms. The hard, cut edges will not appear so later, for they will soften when the felt is fulled.

FULLING BY HAND

There are many alternative ways of fulling felt [Step 17]. Regardless of which you choose, be sure to work on both sides of the batt, unless you want the piece to felt primarily on one side.

A soft, loose felt can be made by simply using an iron. Use a "wool" setting and press in all directions equally. A harder felt can be made by continually rolling the batt in one direction, then unrolling it and rerolling it in the opposite direction. It can be worked with a rolling pin, much as pie dough would be. The felt, like pie dough, should be worked all over. Roll out from the center in a circular motion, or roll back and forth in both a vertical and horizontal direction, and then diagonally. It also works well to roll the batt around the rolling pin, using it as a form to push against. The batt can be rubbed over a washboard, or pounded with a rubber mallet, paddle, potato masher, meat tenderizer, or whatever is available. It can be worked with the feet, as grapes are when wine is made. It's especially nice to do this in the shower: put the basted batt flat on the shower floor

Step 17: Fulling. The hardened batt should be further worked to make a denser, stronger felt. Continue with the same tools and motions you have already used—kneading, rolling, pressing, pounding, and so on. Rolling and rerolling the uncovered batt in a bamboo screen or placemat works well at this stage. Photo Larry Beede.

and use plenty of hot water and soap. This can be done, of course, when you are planning to take a shower anyway. Linda Endres came up with the idea of using the pulsating pressure of a shower massage and Barbara Pickett has tried using the vibrating action of a flat sanding machine. (She completely covers the machine with plastic so water can't get in the motor, but be careful.) Several feltmakers have successfully worked with a mangle.

If it is a large, thick felt that has been thoroughly hardened, you might lay it out flat and roll around on it with your whole body (children love to do this) or you might try to drive over it. Ask a child to ride a bike back and forth all over it, or put it in the driveway and drive the car over it a few times. Several people have even told me they have been thinking about using a steam roller for especially large felts. If you try any of these particularly "violent" fulling methods, keep the batt in its protective covering. If you have already removed it to examine the felt, simply lay it back in without stitching, or put in a few safety pins to hold it in place.

Some people feel it is helpful to let the felt rest at least once during the hardening and fulling process; they leave it alone for half an hour or so. I have been unable to determine conclusively if this really makes a difference. What may be significant is that you, the felter, rest and come back to the work refreshed; or it may be that a time with no agitation gives the fibers a chance to work around each other gently. You might try experimenting with the idea to discover at what point in the process, if any, the rest is most beneficial. Be sure to rinse any soap out of the felt if you leave it for any extended period of time. An alternative suggestion comes from Barbara Pickett, who tells her students to leave the batt in a pan of simmering water while *they* rest. The wool will *not* rest, as it is still subjected to felting conditions.

HARDENING AND FULLING: "STEPPING"
Another method of working the felt, taken from the people of Central Asia, requires more in the way of physical space and set-up. If you have a room with a drain in the floor (many houses have this in the basement) or can work outside on a relatively flat, clean surface, this may work well for you. It's one of the few ways you'll be able to handle a very large piece.

The method involves *stepping* the felt and most contemporary feltmakers have found it works well with large, bamboo-matchstick window screens. (These are often available inexpensively in thrift or second-hand stores.) Imitation bamboo screens, made of plastic, are a little slippery and do not grab hold of the wool as well as the wood, but they will do the job. Large, tightly woven, grass matting also works well. Large fiberglass screens have been used successfully and heavy canvas, like that used by the Turkish feltmakers, is also good.

The batt is laid on the screening material, sometimes in a net covering, but usually directly and with no other backing. The batt is saturated and soaped carefully, so as not to disturb it, then tightly rolled so that wool touches screen or matting (not other wool) at all points. No basting is necessary. The roll is placed on the floor, wet thoroughly (excess water will drain through the floor or be absorbed in the ground) and rolled with the foot. You can do this standing up or sitting down, whichever is most comfortable. Be sure to move your foot along the whole length of the roll, working different areas at different times, so the piece will felt evenly all over. More water and soap can be added at any point and, after the initial hardening, the piece can be unrolled, examined, and repositioned in the screening for further rolling.

If you don't have a floor drain available and it is too cold or otherwise impossible to work outside, it *is* possible to work with the stepping method inside by building a platform that fits over the bathtub. The platform must have drainage holes here and there (about ½ inch in diameter) and must be very sturdy (1-inch plywood, for example), for you will be standing or sitting on top of it as you work.

The stepping method is relatively quick and easy. It is especially effective when the batt is made from drum-carded or commercially prepared wool. It can work successfully with handcarded rolags, but because they are small and are not sewn or pinned in place, they may slip somewhat; the felt is more difficult to control. For this reason, you may find stepping too slippery and frustrating for carefully preplanned, inlaid, or embedded designs. Try a sample piece before you start any major project.

HARDENING AND FULLING: THE WASHING MACHINE

With the washing machine, contemporary feltmakers have a wonderful tool at their disposal. The machine automatically provides heat, water, and pressure or agitation; felt can be made easily, relatively quickly, and without much physical work [Steps 18-20]. The drawbacks of the machine method should be mentioned, though: it is difficult to control the felt; you are not able to feel just what is going on at any moment; the strong agitation may affect the felt in unforeseen ways. It is especially common for the piece to get too hard, too fast. As Lynn Sullivan put it, "You can make felt in less time in the machine, but it's a bit like whipping cream—you have to know when to stop before it turns to butter."

One way to minimize this hard treatment is to prepare the batt a little differently. Cotton is recommended as a backing fabric, for it will hold the batt in place more securely. After basting it to the fabric, roll and work it by hand for a while until it begins to mat together. Then roll it tightly, fold it, and bind it with strong thread or cord. These extra steps are important. If the batt is put in the machine without being initially worked by hand, it may be very weak; if it is put in the machine without the extra rolling and binding, it is likely to come out with holes and lumpy areas. Bind it tightly enough so the roll will stay together when the felt shrinks, but not so tightly that water can't get through or deep indentations remain. Beth Beede has found that a top-loading machine is more apt to tear felt apart than a front-loading machine, so be certain to use these precautions with a top-loading machine.

I like to use the hottest water possible in the washing machine. Some feltmakers choose to use variable-temperature settings such as "hot—cool—hot," but I don't feel it necessary to shock the wool in the machine any more than in working by hand. If there is a gentle or short cycle on the machine, however, it might be easiest on the felt. Some feltmakers also prefer to take the piece out before the spin cycle. (Debra Glanz, in fact, suggests running the felt through the machine two or three times, each time taking

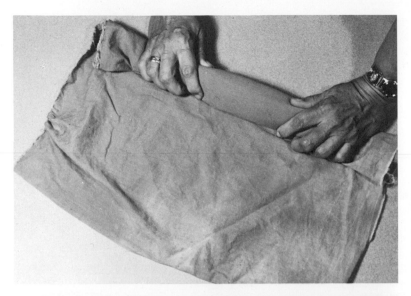

Step 18: Washing Machine Felting.
If you choose to work with a washing machine, tightly roll the somewhat-hardened batt (Step 15) in a piece of cotton fabric. A tight roll is important for an even felt. (Steps 15–17 are not necessary if the machine is used.) Photo Larry Beede.

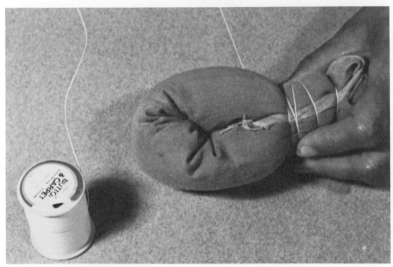

Step 19: Washing Machine Felting.
For extra protection, fold the roll over several times to make an envelope and bind it tightly with strong cord or thread. Photo Larry Beede.

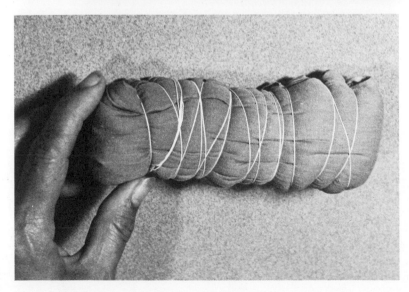

Step 20: Washing Machine Felting.
The bound roll is ready for the washing machine. You may soak it in soapy water before putting it in the machine, but this is not strictly necessary. For a dense felt, use the hottest setting possible and add soap as you would for any load of laundry. For lighter felts, use gentler settings and shorter cycles. Tightly bound this way, the batt can even go in with your regular wash. Photo Larry Beede.

it out before the spin cycle begins.) Other feltmakers choose a different cycle corresponding to the hardness of the felt they are aiming for. Anne Dushanko-Dobek uses a 7-minute cycle and half a tub of water for lightly felted pieces and a 13-minute cycle and a full tub of water for dense felt. Margaret Rhein likes to balance her felt loads with a large sheet. I've had good results without any special precautions—I've put well-bound batts in with my regular laundry, using hot water and a full, regular cycle, and have had no problems.

After felting in the machine, untie and unroll the batt. If it feels hard enough, take it out of the backing fabric and see if it is as dense as you would like. If not, it can be put in the dryer for further fulling (see below) or it can be returned to its backing fabric and put in the washer for another cycle. Never put an uncovered piece of felt in the washing machine; the agitation is intense and likely to tear it apart. Even if this doesn't happen, stray pieces of wool may clog up the machine.

An automatic dryer can be used for both fulling the felt and drying it thoroughly. The dryer will always shrink and harden the piece further (shrinkage will be equal on all sides; in most of my experiments, it was about 1 to 2 inches on all sides of flat rectangular pieces that were about 5 to 12 inches by 15 to 36 inches). Do not use a dryer if your piece is especially soft and delicate or if you want a loose, buoyant felt surface. A thoroughly hardened felt can go through a dryer uncovered, but it is always a good idea to protect it by putting it in a mesh bag. Make the bag out of the mosquito netting suggested for backing fabric, or use the kind of bag sold specifically for protecting fine washables in the washer and dryer.

A note about felting with machines: Beth Beede reasoned that if an automatic washer felted well, an automatic dishwasher might work, too. She tried it, but only got a "mess" as a result. She also tried felting in a pressure cooker and had no luck with that either.

FINISHING THE FELT

If a soap solution or some other lubricating agent has been used, the finished felt must be rinsed. Remove the backing fabric if you have not already done so and hold the felt under running water until all the soap is gone. A dipping in a vinegar rinse may also be helpful, for it will neutralize any soap residue.

The felt can be dyed at this point in any number of different ways, all of which are discussed in Chapter Six. Other finishes might also be applied. In the last chapter we mentioned the kinds of treatments used by industrial feltmakers. I have not investigated these in detail, but if you wish to explore them further and apply them to hand feltmaking, try contacting the felt industry directly. (Addresses are listed in the Appendix.) Lynn Sullivan has adapted one commercial treatment, mothproofing, to her own purposes. Prior to drying her pieces, she puts them in a final hot bath with a 3-percent Eulan solution. If your felt is going to be hung or stored in an enclosed area, this protective treatment would be particularly appropriate.

Felt can be dried in the same ways washed wool is dried: hung in a vertical position, placed on screens, or blown with a fan or hairdryer. A few feltmakers have even tried speeding up the drying process by putting their pieces in the oven on a low setting, but this is a tricky business and I don't recommend it. Even if the felt is made by hand, it can, of course, be dried in the automatic dryer. It can be tossed in for just a few minutes to help remove excess moisture, even when additional fulling is not desirable.

When dry, the felt can be brushed and napped to create a shaggier surface. Teasel, the dried seed heads of the teasel plant, are ideal for this. You can also use the kind of brush sold for grooming dogs and cats, or even a hairbrush.

The opposite effect—a smooth, almost polished surface—can be achieved by shearing, rubbing, sanding, and ironing. Shearing is difficult but worth experimenting with. Use as large a scissors as you can find and hold it completely parallel to and just above the surface of the felt. Grasp any loose fibers and hold them up perpendicular to the felt surface. Move the scissors along in a smooth and rhythmical fashion, clipping the upright fibers as close to the surface as possible.

You can try rubbing as the Turkish feltmakers do: use a flat, smooth stone; a brick covered with cloth so it is not too rough; a pumice stone; a piece of heavy, highly polished wood; a rolling pin; or even a cylindrical plastic drinking glass. Rub it over the felt, applying as much pressure as you can. I find it easiest to rub with a circular motion. Think of this as ironing the felt—removing wrinkles, smoothing, and flattening it. You can also use an actual iron. Lay a damp cloth over the felt or, if the iron is quite clean, iron directly on the felt surface.

Turkish feltmakers in Shiraz singe the felt by passing it over an open flame to burn off any remaining loose fibers. Use this method only with an all-wool or nearly all-wool felt. Wool tends to be self-extinguishing, but other fibers, particularly vegetable fibers, can burn and you may create holes in the felt or, even worse, have a fire on your hands. Have a pan of water within easy reach for extinguishing unwanted flames, even if you are working with pure wool. This treatment may make the felt a little rough, for the singed end of each wool fiber has a tiny knob on the end. A flame on a gas stove, a large dripless candle, or even a blowtorch can be used. Brush the felt thoroughly with your hand after singeing to remove all of the fiber ash.

Sanding very hard felt made of short fibers can be done by hand with fine sandpaper or emery paper, but it might be more effectively done with a hand-held, belt-type sanding machine. The edges of felt can be tacked down to a piece of wood for stability. Experiment with small pieces of felt to see what kind of hand movements are best and how fast the smoothing takes place.

Finally, you can work with the edges of the felt. Sharp or hard edges can be easily made by cutting with a scissors or trimming or bevelling with a single-edge razor or Exacto knife. Soft, uneven, or hairy-looking edges can be made by pulling and teasing the edges out with the fingers. Both techniques can be used in the same piece for an interesting contrast. If the edges are left loose and soft, the felt can be easily joined (seamed) to another piece of felt later. They can be cut and then refelted (thus reshaping the piece, but maintaining the effect of a soft edge) or made to look hard and straight by the insertion of a piece of yarn during the felting process. These techniques are discussed in more detail in the remaining chapters.

CHAPTER FIVE

Forming Techniques with Felt

Up to this point, I have been discussing ways of making plain, flat felt. Some of the most exciting things contemporary feltmakers are exploring, however, involve felt that has been shaped into specific forms. Shaping can be done in many ways. Edges can be felted together, creating built-in seams; *resists* (materials that will not felt themselves) can be inserted in areas of the hardening felt and later removed, leaving flaps, pockets, and hollow areas; surfaces can be manipulated so that certain areas protrude or recede; relatively soft, pliable felt can be shaped over a mold or an armature, or batts can be positioned over other types of molds and literally felted into specific shapes; and fibers can be stuffed into molds to form solid shapes. These techniques can be combined in various ways and a great variety of forms made by felting processes alone. The design possibilities are extended even further by the addition of sewing or glueing operations.

SEAMS AND RESISTS

The principle of making a felt seam is really quite simple. If two flat, rectangular pieces of relatively soft felt are placed side by side so their edges overlap [72] and the pieces are then worked (fulled) further, the edges will felt together or make a seam. The two smaller rectangles will be joined into a single, larger rectangle. Extra carded wool can be placed on this overlapping area as reinforcement, but is not strictly necessary. Any two felt edges can be joined this way.

Now imagine you wish to make a felt tube by folding over the two edges of a rectangular piece, so they overlap to form a seam. If you then fulled the folded piece thoroughly, when you tried to open the finished tube you would not be able to; for not only will the overlapping edges have felted together, but the whole of the tube as well. As John Thomson remarked in 1868:

> The writer has seen a [fulling] millful of [wool stockings used by whale fisherman] whose sides were felted so firmly together, from a neglect of the workmen to turn them inside out, in due time, during the felting operation, that a knife was required to open them, and which actually failed in several instances, so firmly had their two sides grown together; common tearing having no effect whatever, each and every single hair had embraced its neighbors, and their mutual action defied all attempts to open [them].

To create a tubular shape, then, a *resist* must be placed between the two layers of wool during the fulling process. A resist is any

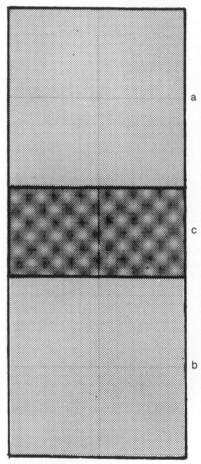

72. Two pieces of soft felt (*a* and *b*) can be joined together (seamed) by overlapping their edges slightly (*c*) and working them together with continued fulling.

material that resists felting, just by keeping two pieces of felt or wool apart as they are worked. The overlapping seams will felt together, but not the whole body of the finished piece.

Tightly woven cloth, heavy paper or cardboard, and leather are all excellent resists. Plastic resists can be satisfactory, but plastic absorbs no water and tends to slip around somewhat under the pressure of felting. Resist materials can be cut to any size and shape.

A simple felt pouch can be made in much the same way as the tube described above, by positioning a resist between two felt batts. The resist should be a little smaller than the batts; it should not extend all the way to the edges of the wool, except on the side where the opening of the pouch will be. This means the wool at three of the edges *will* be allowed to felt into a seam [Step 1]. As I said before, extra wool may be added at these edges to reinforce them. For best results—and the most control—the resist should be removed after a certain degree of hardening and the fabric worked for a while with no other material either inside or outside it. That last little bit of fulling—fine tuning, so to speak—is best done with no impediments. If the resist is cut in a rounded shape rather than a rectangular one, the inside pocket will be rounded as well [73]. The corners of the pouch could then also be cut to form a rounded shape with the same contours.

An even sturdier felt pouch can be made in a similar but slightly more complicated fashion, with the edges folded inside one another [Steps 1–4]. A rectangle with a pocket on either end can be made by positioning a second layer of wool over a resist on the far ends of a batt [74]. A rectangular pouch with a small central opening (a tissue dispenser shape) can be made by covering more of the resist, leaving a tab to pull out after hardening [75]. The possibilities for pouches, tabs, flaps, and hollow areas are endless and, once the principle is understood, they are easily designed.

Hats, as we have seen in Chapters Two and Three, can also be made with the use of resists and felt seams. In most cases where hats are made by hand, a paper or cloth resist is placed between layers of wool or fur, with the fiber extending out beyond the edges of the resist. The fiber is worked so the edges felt together, leaving an open pocket inside and forming a basic conical shape. Felt shoes were made in 19th-century America in essentially the same way: wool batts were put on both sides of a triangular resist of brown paper and the edges folded over and joined together. One corner of the hardened form was later cut off for the opening and the forms pulled and made into shoe shapes on special lasts. In Sweden, shoes were sometimes made over lasts, but at other times they were made by layering batts in an L shape, using a cotton resist between layers, and hardening thoroughly.

Another interesting technique is sometimes used in Sweden for fashioning felt seams: seams are stitched directly through the batt with a soft, loosely spun, wool yarn. After thorough fulling, the thread actually felts in and is nearly invisible.

Louis Levine, who visited an Iranian feltmaker's workshop in 1973, commissioned a traditional felt coat and watched it being made. His description of the process of shaping the coat, published in *Studies in Textile History,* is interesting to us at this

73. A resist can also be placed in the middle of a batt. After the piece is felted, the top edge can be cut open to expose a hollow pocket.

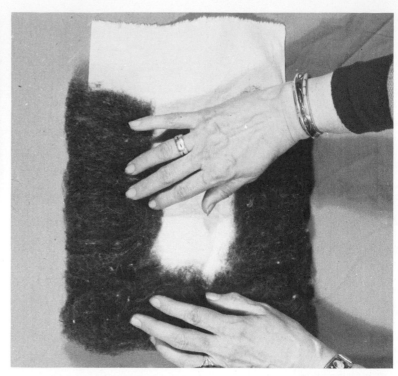

Step 1. (Above) Put a resist over a prepared batt, leaving several inches uncovered on three sides. Photo Larry Beede.

Step 2. (Right) Fold the edges of the batt over the resist, envelope fashion. Photo Larry Beede.

Step 3. (Above) Place the folded-over batt on another batt, fold side down. The second batt can be another rectangle, or a T shape as illustrated. Photo Larry Beede.

Step 4. (Right) Fold the edges of the second batt over the first, already folded batt. Put the whole package in a backing material and continue felting as usual. Since all seamed edges are especially well reinforced with this method, it produces a strong sturdy pouch. Photo Larry Beede.

78

point because it illustrates how seams and resists can be used to make a shaped felt garment.

The feltmaker covered a large tarp with loosened wool and shaped it into a cross form, with one side of the cross slightly wider than the other [76]. The cross-shaped batt was rolled in the tarp and hardened, primarily with a stepping motion. It was then unrolled, folded in half (thus forming a T shape), and straightened. A small hole was made at the top of the T—the neck—by pulling apart the fibers and folding them under. Reinforcing wool was added to this area. The extra width at the back of the T (the back of the coat) was also loosened by being pulled slightly and, when loose, folded over the front of the T (the front of the coat), thus forming a tubular shape. Extra wool was also added at these side seams. (The coat had already been thoroughly hardened and a resist was not used between the back and front of the garment in this case. It would be wise to use a resist if you were following this general idea, however.) The armholes of the coat were also torn open and shaped in a similar fashion.

The piece was then fulled: it was soaped, rolled, folded, and refolded in opposite directions for hours. The feltmaker then opened the bottom of the coat with a knife and climbed inside. "By . . . pulling on the hem, he gave the garment its final flared form, with the bottom wider than the shoulders." The hem was made by cutting the felt in a straight line, the front opening was made by cutting a slit from the neckline to the hem.

The principles of making a shaped batt, folding it in half, making seams by folding one edge over another, and cutting into either a soft or finished hard felt, all illustrated here, can be adapted to other projects that need shaping.

Another interesting anecdote relevant to the subject of resists comes from the Greek geographer Strabo, describing India in the days of Alexander the Great. R.J. Forbes, in *Studies in Ancient Technology,* quotes him as follows:

> [When the Indians] saw sponges in use among the Macedonians, they made imitations by sewing tufts of wool through and through with hair and light cords and threads and . . . after compressing [the wool] into felt, they drew out the inserts and dyed the sponge-like felt.

74. (Left) A resist can be placed at one end of a batt, forming a pocket at that point only. There is no harm in leaving a long resist—it's easier to remove after hardening. Photo Larry Beede.

75. (Above) Always leave a resist tab to pull out after felting, no matter what shape you are working with. Photo Larry Beede.

It is difficult to understand why the hair and threads were not thoroughly entrapped in the felt, but we must remember that Strabo may not have really understood the felting process and this could be an incomplete description. In any case, a similar "sponge-like felt" could easily be made today with a different kind of resist. Plastic drinking straws knotted on both ends, for example, would not get caught in the wool and would be long enough to be pulled out easily after felting.

Strabo's anecdote reminds us that resists can be used in a wide variety of ways, limited only by our imagination. Any material can be kept from felting by a resist. A sisal rope, for example, might be caught in the wool fibers and thus trapped in the finished felt in most areas, but kept free in a few places where it had been wrapped or tied with a piece of cloth resist. The wrapping could be applied at regular intervals and a design similar to a tie-dye or ikat pattern might even be made in this way. Ideas almost generate themselves as you experiment. After working with felt seams and resists for a while, you will probably find new and intriguing ways to use them.

FELTING OVER MOLDS

Felt is easily moldable in certain shapes. No angular, geometric forms with corners or straight lines will really "take"—molded felt does tend to become round—but soft, organic forms, particularly concave and convex configurations, can be successfully and satisfyingly worked with.

There are two basic ways to mold felt: by putting somewhat hardened but still soft felt over a mold and then forming it, or by wrapping and shaping wool batts around the mold and hard-

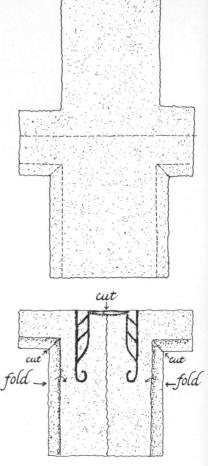

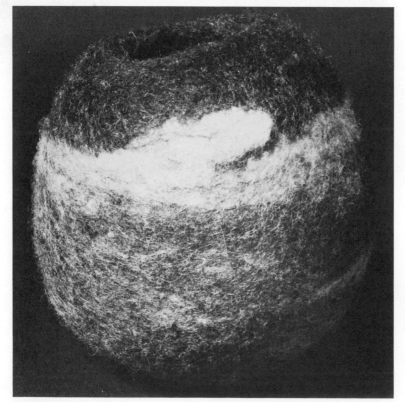

76. (Above) Felt coat made in 1973 by Mashd Heshmat Bakhtiari in the village of Seh Gabi, central western Iran. The batt was laid out in the shape of a cross and, after hardening, folded over into the shape of a T. Extra width on the back of the coat was folded over the front to make the side and arm seams. The design on the front was inlaid after hardening. Illustration Jeanne Freer.

77. (Left) Untitled bowl by Carolyn Bowler, natural wools, 6″ high (15.2 cm). Bowler's containers are formed over foam rubber and felted in the washing machine. The direction in which the wool was wrapped around the mold is evident. Courtesy the artist.

Plate 1. (Right) Felt saddle covering unearthed from the first Pazirik tomb. Felts of different colors were sewn together to make this magnificent piece. The seat of a covering like this was often stuffed. Courtesy The Hermitage, Leningrad.

Plate 2. Detail of *Secrets* by Margaret Rhein, demonstrating the artist's use of color in a tie-dye fashion. Photo Marty Mulligan.

Plate 3. Detail of *Heather Color Wave* by Pat Boutin Wald. Strips of color cascade gracefully in this rainbowlike piece. Acid dyes were used for the colors and the pieces were stitched together after felting. Courtesy the artist.

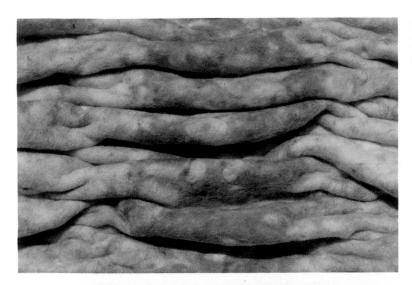

Plate 4. The warm, soft, sensuous qualities of felt are evident in this detail of Kristy L. Higby's *Soft Shell*. See also [94]. Photo Rick Gast.

Plate 5. (Above) Detail of *Woven Worms* by Pat Spark. One of the qualities of felt is the way individual wool fibers work their way into one another—and into other areas. Here, gray fibers move over the dense brown "worm" forms that emerge from the felt surface. Courtesy the artist.

Plate 6. (Left) Rich textures and colors make *Terra Madre Too* (detail shown here), by Marleah Drexler Mac-Dougal, an involving piece. Many artists find felt associated with images of the earth. Courtesy the artist.

Plate 7. (Left) *A Chair by the Window* by Deborah Kaufman, 63″ × 32″ (160 × 81 cm). The delightful details in Kaufman's pieces are made by inlaying predyed wool and yarns before felting. The natural distortions that occur in the felting process are taken into consideration when the pieces are designed. Courtesy the artist.

Plate 8. (Right) Kristy L. Higby's *Sweeter Fare* is a wonderful illustration of the rich effects possible with layered colors in felt, 15″ × 23″ (38 × 58.5 cm). Multilayered felt was cut into strips, rolled, and stitched together. Photo Rick Gast.

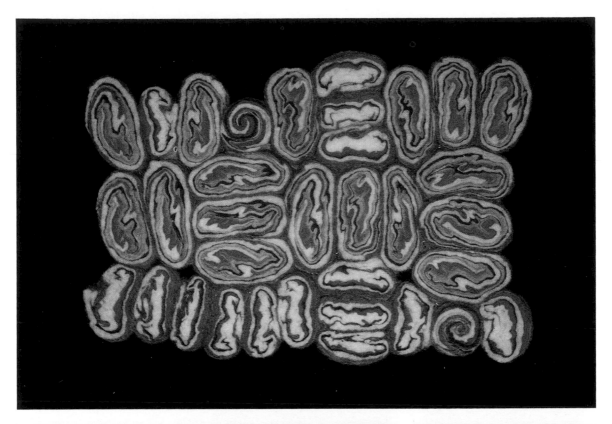

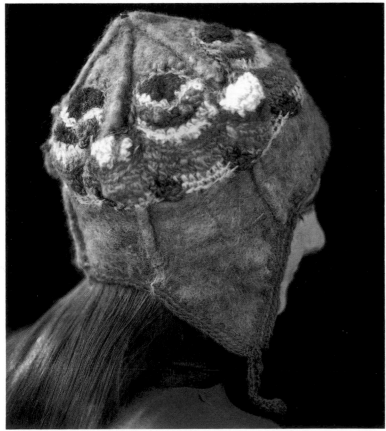

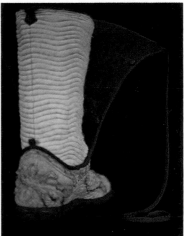

Plate 9. (Left) Helmet by Denise Welch-May. Felt and crochet are combined in this fanciful and functional hat. Photo Ted Degener.

Plate 10. (Above) *First Felted, Then Lasted Boots* by Gaza Bowen. Felt is quilted to a backing fabric and attached to a strong sole, so the boots may be worn. Photo Amtul Hannan.

Plates 11 and 12. Untitled landscapes by Lynda Lowe Oren: 56″ × 100″ (142 × 254 cm) above, 51″ × 57″ (129.8 × 144.8 cm) left. Oren's richly colored, monumental pieces are fleece-dyed with acid dyes; as many as 70 colors are used on one piece. She lays carded wool or, where defined edges are desired, lightly felted wool on top of a four- or five-layered batt. Oren is probably the foremost felt colorist; her painterly approach is 'unique. Courtesy the artist.

Plate 13. (Opposite page, top) Detail of *Ocean* by Deone Tremblay. The colors and forms of this piece are most effective in evoking the sea. Children helped harden it by rolling over it—see [168]. Courtesy the artist.

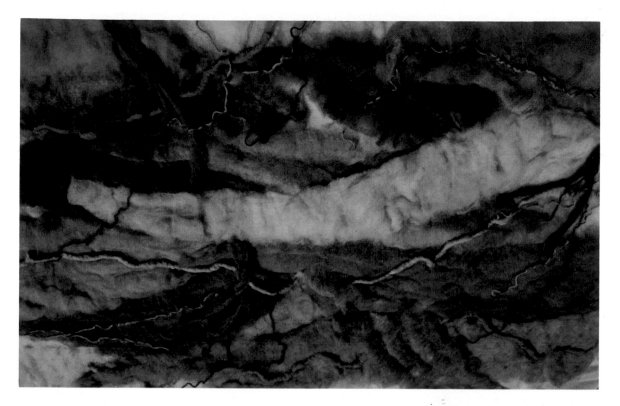

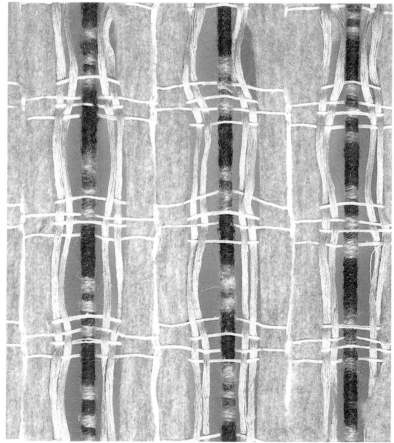

Plate 14. (Above) *Slab Pot* by Barbara Setsu Pickett, 5½″ high (14 cm). Layers of color are also evident in this molded form. Another artist, Pat Spark, remarked that the possibilities of the cut felt edge had great appeal for her. She noted that the artist could refine it after felting, "as a potter can with leather-hard clay." Courtesy the artist.

Plate 15. (Left) Detail of *Felt Construction #3* by Katarina Weslien. To make this piece, Weslien resist dyed yarns ikat-fashion and wrapped them around wooden dowels. The dowels and carded fleece were then woven into a linen warp and the whole piece placed in screening and felted by stepping. Photo Harriet Hartigan.

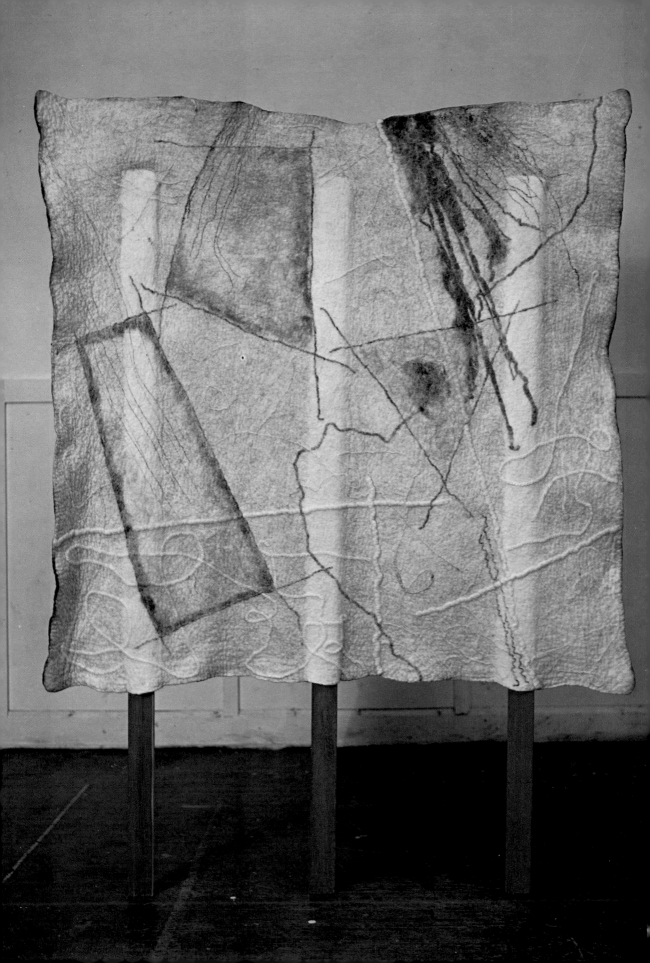

ening and fulling them directly on it. The first method has one major disadvantage: it can be difficult to get the flexibility and control needed to form particular shapes. It has the advantage, however, of lessening the likelihood of weak areas or slippage. Felting wool batts directly on a mold can be tricky to do properly, but the fact that the fiber is actually hardening in a specific shape assures its smooth contour and close adherence to that shape.

All kinds of materials can function as molds, as long as they will stand up to the pressure of being worked with the felt. Wooden molds were used by the Scythians and the Scandinavians, but it is generally easiest to work on a mold with some amount of resilience. (It should not, on the other hand, actually lose or change its shape.) Contemporary feltmakers have tried working over bundles of wadded-up cloth, Styrofoam, foam rubber, polyurethane, balloons, balls, and plastic bowls [77, 78]. While different people have their own favorite mold materials, what works best often depends on how they arrange the fiber, what kind of backing material they cover it with, and how they work with it. A look at some specific forming processes should illustrate how molding works and indicate ways the basic steps can be varied. Once you understand the process, you can experiment to find the appropriate mold for any particular project.

When working with wool batts, one of the simplest and most basic molded forms is a small cup or bowl. This can be made relatively easily over a sock (cotton or nylon—not wool) stuffed with several washcloths. Push the washcloths very tightly into the foot of the sock, filling it approximately to the top of the heel.

Plate 16. (Opposite page) *Sentinel I* by Joan Livingstone, 67″ × 52″ × 19½″ (170 × 132 × 49.5 cm). See also [132]. Photo George Crary. Courtesy The Hadler-Rodriguez Galleries, New York.

78. Untitled bowl by Carolyn Bowler, natural wools, 6½″ high (16.5 cm). The vertical ridges on this piece were formed by tight wrapping of the form during the felting process. Courtesy the artist.

Then, carefully wrap carded wool batts or rolags (batts are broader and therefore much easier to work with here) around the sock. Ideally, these should be built up in layers around the sock form, just as layers of batts are built up at right angles to one another for a flat felt piece. It is sometimes difficult to hold the wool around the mold at this stage, but as it is important to position it carefully, keep working at it [79, 80]. It may help to have the wrapped mold sit in another bowl. The top of the sock will be emerging, uncovered, out of the wool-wrapped ball; the top of the sock will serve as a resist at the opening of the cup or bowl.

The wrapped sock should then be further wrapped in a backing material. This wrapping must be tight enough to keep the wool securely in place and it must hold up to a great deal of pressure. One possibility is to use a piece of tightly woven cotton sheeting, tied on with cord drawn in all directions over the sock. This method works well, but if it has been wrapped tightly enough to hold the fiber in place it may leave indentations on the bowl—lines like the meridians on a globe. In exploring this technique, Susan Marie Cunningham substituted rubber bands for cord. These held the fiber in place, but left indentations that were especially pronounced. Instead of cotton backing cloth, an ace bandage or some similar elastic cloth can be used (this has the advantage of being able to contract as the wool shrinks), or the whole ball can be put in a stretchable nylon stocking (support hose works even better than regular nylons). These methods may be combined: the wool-wrapped sock can be covered with a piece of cotton that in turn is covered by an ace bandage or stocking.

Felt the whole wrapped ball, using hand rolling, kneading, or pressing motions, or use the action of the washing machine. A clothes dryer can be used for even further fulling. Remove the protective casing material and pull the washcloths out of the sock opening. Gently peel the felt away from the sock. You can continue working the bowl or cup form without the mold—rewet it if necessary and keep fulling and shaping it further.

As I have said, felt has a tendency to become round. There is no need to worry, therefore, if the mold only approximates a bowl and is not truly spherical. It is actually more difficult to produce an ovoid or elongated shape. If you want a mold of this shape, experiment with ways of exaggerating the elongation of the original mold and stuff the wool in very tightly so it can't round out.

One of the critical elements that makes the stuffed-sock mold work is the fact that there is built-in resist at the opening of the bowl. If you choose to work over a spherical mold, decide whether or not you want an area to be left unfelted for the opening. If you do, be sure to place a resist there. You may also choose to felt the bowl as a sphere and cut it open after felting. This brings up the second critical element: whether or not the mold will be removable after the felting is complete. If you want to be able to take it out, you must leave a big enough opening, work with a mold that can either come out in sections (for example, a number of wadded-up washcloths) or deflate (such as a strong balloon), or be willing to cut the mold apart (this works well with rubber balls). In Sweden, heavy felt socks are worked over a mold made of two wooden forms that hook together.

79. Margaret Rhein makes bowl forms by wrapping carded wool around a tightly rolled nylon sock. The wool must be carefully positioned so the bowl will be smooth and even. Photo Kathy Hume.

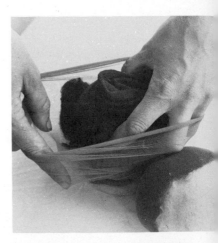

80. Margaret Rhein's wrapped socks are secured in a nylon stocking. She makes several bowl forms at once; after each one is tightly secured, she ties an overhand knot and moves on to the next. Photo Kathy Hume.

This idea—molds made of several pieces that fit together—is an intriguing solution.

The instructions for felting around a ball [Steps 1–8] illustrate the process of working over a mold. They also illustrate the way the form can be placed in a larger bowl during wrapping and the way wool is cross-lapped in a circular pattern. Note that the appearance of the bowl or ball will be affected by the direction of the wool on the top layer. Carolyn Bowler's bowls [77, 78] illustrate this point clearly.

Susan Marie Cunningham doesn't usually wash fleece when she makes a flat piece of felt, but recommends doing so when molding felt. I think this is a good rule of thumb. Remember, with a mold inside the wool it will be more difficult for the lanolin and dirt to be worked out during felting.

One feltmaker, Rhoda Asnien, uses a slightly different molding technique. She stitches wool batts between two pieces of muslin and wraps the "sandwich" around a plastic bowl. The whole package—bowl covered by muslin-covered batts—is hardened and fulled in the washing machine and dryer. Because the wool is not directly touching the mold, it may be somewhat more difficult to control the shape with this technique, but it is worth experimenting with.

81. *Felt Basket* by Caroline Von Kleeck Beard, 15″ x 14″ at the base (38.1 x 35.6 cm). A graceful, unusual, molded form in purple wool. Gold foil "burrs" complete the piece. Courtesy the artist.

82. This head, 10″ high (25.4 cm), is part of *Charlie*, a performing mask by Beth Beede. A sphere was felted over a ball mold to the soft-felt stage and the features then formed in it. Ears, eyebrows, lips, and nose arch were pinched in the felt and basted tightly with heavy thread. The nose was further forced out with the aid of more hot water and was stuffed with a small Styrofoam ball. The whole piece was fulled heavily and, after drying, the stitches removed. To complete the mask, a helmet and neckpiece were added later. Photo Larry Beede.

83. Untitled mask by Beth Beede, 66″ long with raffia (167.3 cm), formed over a ball. White cowrie shells and natural raffia were applied after the molding was complete. The mask has been used in dance performances. Photo Larry Beede.

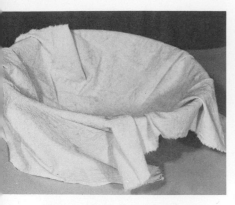

Step 1. (Above) Line a bowl with a
large piece of muslin or sheeting material. Fabric should hang over the
edges of the bowl. Photo Larry
Beede.

Step 2. (Right) Position carded wool
batts over the sheeting material. It
should fill the bowl thoroughly (extra
wool in the bottom is a good idea)
and overlap well at all points. Photo
Larry Beede.

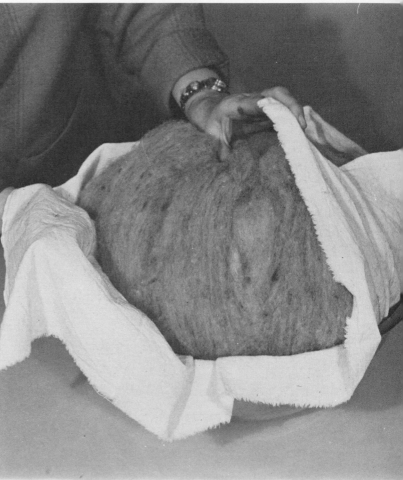

Step 3. (Above) Put an extra roll of
carded wool along the rim of the
bowl. Place a hollow beach ball or
child's ball in the center. Photo Larry
Beede.

Step 4. (Right) Draw the fiber up over
the ball, entirely covering it at all
points. Draw the sheeting material up
over the fiber. Photo Larry Beede.

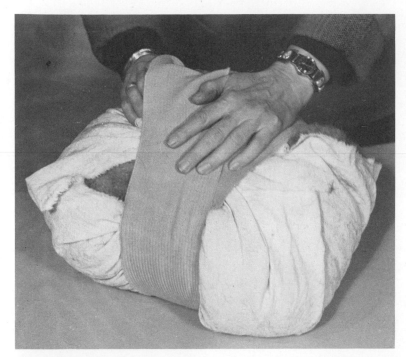

Step 5. (Left) Secure the wool batts and cotton sheeting around the ball by wrapping an Ace® bandage or similar material around it. The elastic will tighten as the felt shrinks and will leave no ridges or indentations. Photo Larry Beede.

Step 6. (Above) When the ball is entirely wrapped with the Ace® bandage, secure it with safety pins. Photo Larry Beede.

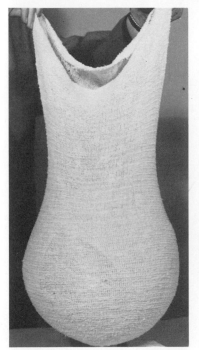

Step 7. (Above) For extra protection, put the whole wrapped ball in a cheesecloth bag. Tie it closed, saturate thoroughly, and full in the dryer. Photo Larry Beede.

Step 8. When the cloth coverings are removed, a felt-covered ball will be revealed. The ball can be returned, uncovered, to the dryer for extra fulling, but it might be a good idea to put it back in the cheesecloth bag for protection. The rubber ball will remain inside the felt unless it is cut into and removed. Photo Larry Beede.

The other basic forming method, as I have stated, involves shaping a piece of flat felt over a mold. Laura Basanta makes bowl shapes, for example, by putting felt over a mold and alternately steaming it with an iron and shaping it with her hands, stretching it continually over the mold form. Her method is, of course, very similar to that of the traditional hatmaker. Even today, women's hats are professionally shaped in a similar manner. Felt is formed into basic hatlike forms at a commercial hat factory and shipped to people who specialize in turning them into fashionable shapes. They work with steam irons, molding the felt while it is moist and wet. Beth Beede began experimenting with this kind of forming by shaping felt over a Styrofoam head (the kind used to display hats and wigs). She cut slits and stretched the felt for rounded eyes and mouth, and carefully steamed, pinched, and stretched the area around the nose. The result is reminiscent of Japanese Noh masks, with subtle shapes and rather flattened features [Steps 1–3]. In order to get more finely chiseled features, the mold would have to have been much more exaggerated.

Traditionally, Swedish mittens were worked the same way: the felt was first semi-hardened as a flat piece and then fulled directly on the hand. This tradition has given me the idea of molding felt over other body parts—the feet for shoes, and heads for hats. If the felting was done directly over a person's head, the mold would certainly be an ideal shape; a tight-fitting bathing cap could be worn to keep human hair out of the wool. Another alternative would be to make a mold with fast-setting, plaster-impregnated bandages—the kind used by sculptor George Segal in his castings of life-size figures. The molding would be done over the mold rather than the head in this case, eliminating the need for the model to stand still during hardening. Some kind of foam or stuffing material would probably also have to be placed inside the cast-bandage mold for resistance or something to push against; without this, the bandages might distort or even give way. I have not actually tried to do any molding on the human body, but the idea intrigues me and should be workable.

FORMING WITH SUPPORTING STRUCTURES, SEWING, AND GLUEING

For some projects, it will be impractical or too difficult to achieve the desired effect by forming directly with the felt. This may be the time to call on other supports or armatures, or to utilize a variety of sewing and glueing techniques. These can be used either instead of or in addition to the molding techniques.

Nancy Algrim is a feltmaker who has done a good deal of work with armatures made of cord and wire [84–87]. She stitches pieces of dyed felt carefully around the wire and subsequently bends and twists them into fluid, organic shapes. Each piece is made of a number of armatures—single armatures form the individual petals of a flower, for example [86]. Algrim's armatures are usually used at the edges of the felt, but consider working with them in other places as well. In all cases, the armatures remain in the finished piece. Molly Fowler, a Connecticut weaver, has also made a number of figures with wire armatures. Her bird [88] is reminiscent of the Scythian swan illustrated in Chapter Two. Both are sewn together and stuffed.

Supporting structures can also be directly trapped in the felt.

Step 1. Use a relatively thin, pliable felt. Soften it by moistening it with steam and stretch it around the mold. Photo Larry Beede.

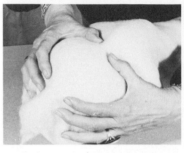

Step 2. Hold the softened, stretched felt over the mold. If possible, pin it to the mold (straight pins could be pushed right into this Styrofoam face, for example). Continually pull and work the felt around the mold, using the steam iron to help with the shaping. Push the tip of the iron directly into the concave spaces— here, the junction of nose and cheek. Cut negative spaces like the eyes and mouth. Photo Larry Beede.

Step 3. Keep shaping and pulling until the desired form is achieved. Use the iron to help dry the piece in its newly formed position. Note how the finished shape only echoes the original mold. Photo Larry Beede.

84. (Top Left) *Blue Iris* by Nancy Algrim, 33″ x 24″ (83.8 x 60.9 cm). Silk is felted to the surface on the bottom petals of this magnificent flower. The felt is shaped over wire armatures with great skill. *Blue Iris* can sit on its own Plexiglas stand (as it does here) or hang suspended on nylon line. Algrim likes "the surrealistic feeling of it floating in space," which reminds her of "some kind of sea creature." Courtesy the artist.

85. (Left) Detail of *The Hostess* by Nancy Algrim. The piece is yellow and red, with a white and gold pistil and stamen in the center. Courtesy the artist.

86. (Top) *Perfection* by Nancy Algrim is made of an exceptionally fine, white, Romney-Lincoln crossbred fleece, 36″ x 36″ x 8″ (91.4 x 91.4 x 20.3 cm). It is one of the artist's favorite pieces; she likes its rich texture, creamy white color, depth, and softness. Courtesy the artist.

87. (Above) Detail of *Perfection* by Nancy Algrim.

88. Detail of a formed and stuffed bird by Molly Fowler, 42″ x 25″ (106.6 x 63.5 cm). The piece, in white, blues, grays, and black, was stitched over wire armatures. Courtesy the author.

Heavy ropes caught between wool layers near the edges of the felt, for example, may serve as a stabilizing element, even a frame. This embedding technique is discussed more fully in Chapter Seven.

Stitched seams can be used effectively in a number of ways. If they are stitched and then turned inside out, as seams on most fabrics are, a distinct rounded ridge will be created. This ridge can be used intentionally—it is an interesting element, for example, in the base of Melonie Rufty's *Ceremonial Soul Basket* [89]. Because a cut felt edge is sharp and nonfraying, however, seams do not have to be turned inside out. Instead, they can be used to highlight the edge and the density of the felt. Sherold Barr's *Moonlite Currents* [92] and Pat Boutin Wald's *Heather Color Wave* [Plate 3] do this successfully. *Moonlite Currents* also illustrates another point: hard linear edges, which are practically impossible to achieve with molded felt, are easy to achieve with cut and stitched felt. As the hard edge is one of the characteristics unique to cut felt, it is appropriate and effective to exploit it.

The fact that felt is a fabric, of course, means it is drapable. It has a fair amount of body and so will not fall into a large number of soft folds, but it *will* respond in a flexible fashion. Like any other fabric, it can be successfully gathered, pleated, bound, rolled, folded, laced, compressed, and so forth. As can be seen here [94–97], most pieces that utilize these techniques are best made with a relatively soft felt.

Quilting or stitching is also very effective on felt. Because felt is a spongy material that compresses well, the stitches function as a sculptural device. The surface takes on new depth and life, defined by the planes of the stitching. The effect can be similar to that of stitching on stuffed nylon stockings or muslin, so popular with soft sculptors today. The dimensional quality of the felt can, of course, be further enhanced by additional padding or stuffing.

The stitching may be used as a linear element to create free-form or representational designs—see Gloria Welniak's *The Patriarch* [99]—or to follow regular lines or patterns. Gaza Bowen's *First Felted, Then Lasted Boot* [Plate 10] indicates the kind

89. *Ceremonial Soul Basket* by Melonie Rufty, wool, pearls, feathers, 9″ high (22.9 cm). This small container evokes a contemplative mood. The rounded base (formed by turning a stitched seam inside out) is an interesting contrast to the cut edge on the lid. Courtesy the artist.

90. Detail of an untitled piece by Patricia Townsend. White felt squares are further marked off into stitched grids and zippers are inserted randomly along some of the seams. The piece changes as zippers are opened and closed, as the negative spaces and depths vary. Photo Allen Smith.

91. *Box for a Long-Stemmed Rose* by Meg Cantor, 18″ long (45.7 cm). Flat and molded felt is here stitched into a box form. There are wonderful details on this piece: rose petals embedded in the wool batt bleed subtle color into the felt; a lining of silk organza is printed with a photocopy transfer of the rose itself; gold-painted thorns and a dry rose stem are attached to the outside of the box. The dried roses are real. Courtesy the artist.

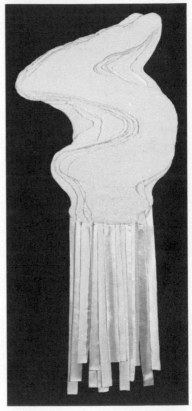

92. (Above) *Moonlite Currents* by Sherold Barr, 72″ x 32″ (180.3 x 81.3 cm). Layers of natural felt are superimposed and set off against one another by white satin. Courtesy the artist.

93. (Left) Detail of *Braided Rivers* by Sherold Barr; the entire wall hanging is 62″ x 17″ (157.5 x 43.2 cm). Barr conceives of her work as aerial views. Courtesy the artist.

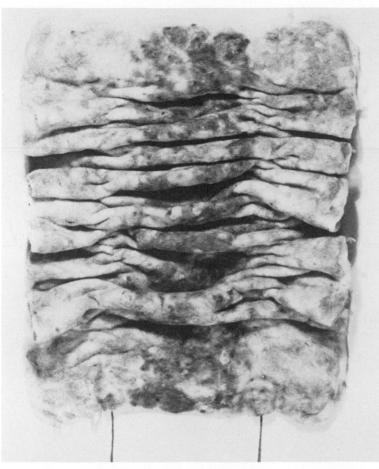

94. (Left) *Soft Shell* by Kristy L. Higby, 21" x 16" (53.3 x 40.6 cm). Relatively soft felt is gathered in this classically simple piece. A rose color is blended with the natural white wool. See also [Plate 4]. Photo Rick Gast.

95. (Below) *Some Get the Marrow Bone* by Kristy L. Higby, dyed and carded fleece wrapped in felt and bound with linen thread, 24" x 13" (61 x 33 cm). The colors are as soft and gentle as the wool itself. Photo Rick Gast.

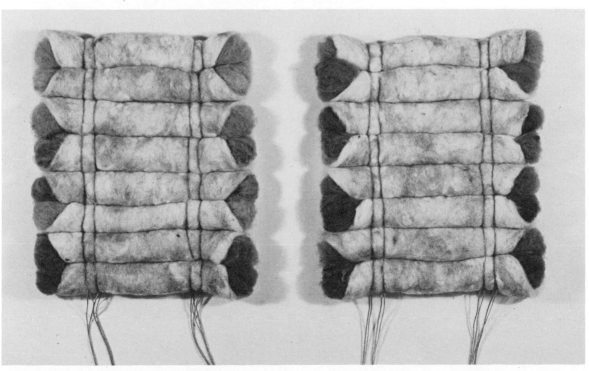

96. *Grey Study* by Karen Van Derpool, each module 17″ x 15″ x 1″ (43.2 x 38.1 x 2.5 cm). Long cylinders were tightly tied at regular intervals before felting to achieve the effect of links. Photo John Wesley.

97. (Above) Detail of *The Search* by Deborah McMahon. This interesting piece is made in five layers: wool felt; stitched and gathered cotton; wool felt; stitched, fringed cotton; and thin wool felt. The piece hints of archaeological finds and hidden messages. Courtesy the artist.

98. (Right) *Formation* by Beth Beede, 36″ x 24″ (91.4 x 61 cm). Soft, flat felt was gathered with dental floss over Styrofoam balls and fulled further, creating a puckered, sphere-filled surface. The balls remain in the finished piece, but the dental-floss ties are completely hidden in the felt. Photo Larry Beede.

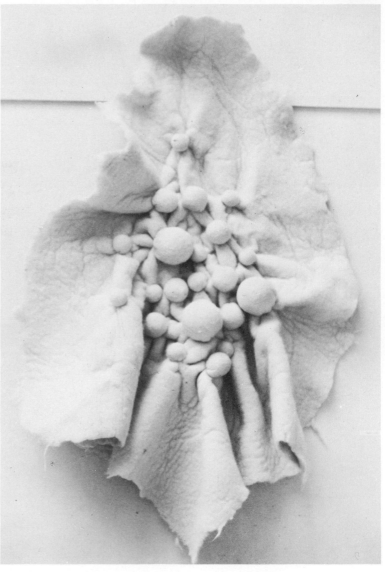

100

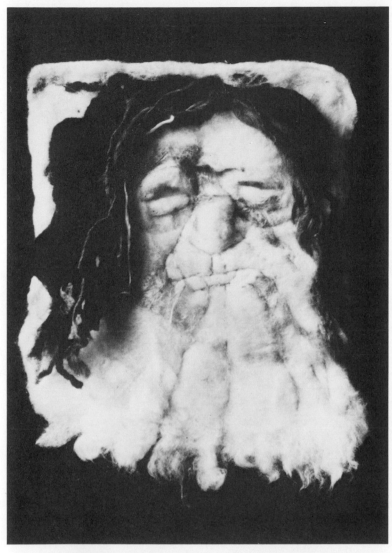

99. *The Patriarch* by Gloria Welniak, 14″ x 12″ (35.6 x 30.5 cm). Felt is stitched and manipulated into the figure of an old man; dark wool is worked in for shading and for hair. This is one of a series of "memorial" images. Courtesy the artist.

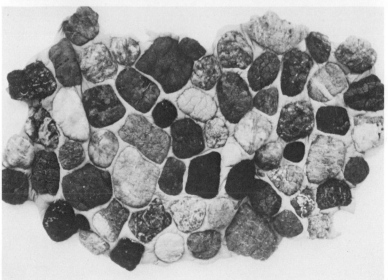

100. *Stone Wall* by Georgia Stegmeier, 42″ x 84″ x 1″–8″ thick (107 x 215.8 x 2.5–20.3 cm). Felt "stones" are quilted in a muslin "mortar." Extra padding is added where necessary. Courtesy the artist.

of sensual quality these linear patterns can take on. I am reminded of the feelings and contours of a freshly plowed field on a rolling terrain. To my knowledge, no one is really exploring this technique as an end in itself, but it presents quite interesting possibilities.

Stitches can usually be made fairly unobtrusively in the felt surface, but if for some reason they are undesirable or difficult to execute, it is also possible to glue pieces of felt together. An all-purpose white glue like Sobo or Elmer's works well, as long as it is not applied too thickly. Epoxies are also very good. Remember that felt is very absorbent and will require a great deal of glue in many cases. Because most glues promote eventual fiber deterioration, the long-term effects of any of them may be harmful. Safest are those glues that are acid-free and have a neutral pH value, such as the methyl-cellulose or wheat-paste glues fine bookbinders and art framers use (see TALAS in Supplier's List).

FELTING WITHIN MOLDS: SOLID SHAPES

Felt can also be formed *inside* a mold. There are built-in limitations to this technique, for the mold must allow water, lubricating agent (if any), and air to flow through freely, and only certain shapes will form successfully. Wonderful effects are possible, however, within these limitations.

The easiest, most natural form to make in a mold is a solid sphere. Like the mold for the cup shape discussed previously, the mold for a ball need not be perfectly spherical, for the felt will become round by its very nature. Wool and other fibers can be stuffed inside a nylon stocking, plastic mesh bag, or sock, or they can be wrapped in a cloth and tied tightly with string. The wool must be carded or loosened well before it is stuffed and compressed in the mold, as it must felt evenly throughout. Tangled or knotted fibers may create holes or breaks because they haven't felted properly. (Again, these breaks—a form of negative space—may also be used consciously for particular effects.)

Generally, felt balls and other similar solid shapes are so dense they are difficult to felt thoroughly by hand; they are best made in the washing machine and/or dryer. The dryer works well by itself; if the wool and the mold are thoroughly saturated and securely tied, the heat and tumbling action will felt the ball with no other agitation or pressure. If the dryer is not used at all, the ball will take a very long time to dry completely.

The density of the ball depends on a number of factors. These include whether or not the wool is washed (I strongly recommend that it is); the length of the wool fiber (a very short fiber will make a much denser ball); how tightly the fiber is stuffed in the mold, and how tightly the mold is tied (remember, the wool will compress a great deal when wet; if possible, wet it before tying or closing the mold); and how long it is hardened and fulled. The length of the fiber and the tightness of the stuffing and tying are the most important of these variables, for even after going through a very hot dryer for an hour and a half, loosely stuffed balls will not get any denser [Steps 1–2].

If a strong thread is run through the ball before felting and left hanging outside the mold, you will have a cord with which to hang or suspend the ball [103]. Margaret Rhein sometimes works with a series of balls, knotted one after another in a single nylon stocking. One thread runs through them all and they are invisibly connected after the felting is complete.

You are no doubt wondering what other kinds of shapes can successfully be made in a mold. The most important thing to remember, again, is that hard angular shapes will become soft and rounded; straight edges will not stay hard and straight. If you were to construct a pyramid-shaped mold out of some stiff porous material, for example, the wool would pull in from the corners and seek a circular shape. A pyramid would be better made by sewing together four flat triangular pieces. Certain shapes might also be made by cutting into very thick felt. If you wanted to make long, solid square poles, perhaps 2 inches square and 2 feet long, for example, it might be possible to make a long 2-inch-thick rectangle and cut it (preferably with a band saw for a very sharp edge) into strips. Another alternative would be to stitch the poles together, much as the pyramid was stitched: four long pieces could be sewn together, with right angles at each seam, to form a rectangle.

A long, thin, sausagelike shape can successfully be formed in a mold but here, too, expect a certain degree of drawing-in, rounding, and shrinkage. In other words, the sausage will probably become shorter and fatter than the mold. To make a felt sausage, sew a cloth tube—wider than the felt tube you are aiming for—or stitch a seam down the length of a nylon stocking to make, in effect, a very narrow stocking. Stuff the mold very tightly with loosened fiber [104]. You can use a smooth stick or some other

Step 1. Stuff a nylon stocking very tightly with carded wool. (Use a variety of colors and textures for a variety of effects in the finished balls.) Saturate the stuffed stocking in water with a little vinegar added to it and shake it up and down so the fiber settles in a solid mass and the excess water drains out. Photo Larry Beede.

Step 2. Tie the stocking tightly with an overhand knot just above the ball. Several balls can be made in the same stocking; knot them one above another. Photo Larry Beede.

long-handled tool to help tamp the fiber down. A doughnut-shaped mold can be made by stitching the ends of the sausage mold together.

I spent a great deal of time trying to make a solid felt hand by using a variety of glove molds, but in every case the fingers tended to become round and to separate from the palm. The palm itself got much too fat and spherical as well. I tried putting sticks inside the fingers as an armature, hoping they would keep the wool connected at the juncture of fingers and palm, but during the fulling action in the dryer, the sticks worked themselves down into the palm of the hand and the fingers still split off. The fingers were lovely shapes in themselves; the shorter ones, especially, were like solid wool cocoons, which were very evocative. I was frustrated, though, by what seemed to be simply a technical problem. I next tried making an armature with pipe cleaners, this time following the outline of the whole hand. Although the fingers did stay attached to the palm, the overall distortion was even worse. The hand was also tinged with a brown color—rust from the pipe-cleaner core. I finally resolved the problem as best I could by leaving the mold in the dryer for only a few minutes. This was enough time to set the shape, but not enough for the tumbling action to bend the fingers toward the palm, thus severing them at the joint. Even here, the palm was unnaturally rounded and the whole surface had breaks throughout [106]. These had formed at many points where different handfuls of fiber had been stuffed into the mold. I have related this project in detail because it highlights some of the problems that arise when unusual solid molds are utilized [107].

103. Felt balls made in nylon stockings. A single stocking can be used for a whole series of balls. Photo the author.

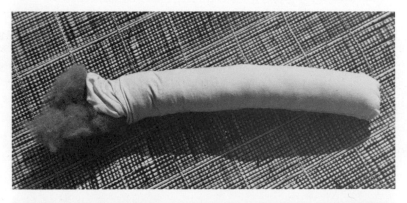

104. A piece of cotton sheeting was stitched into a sausage-shape mold and stuffed tightly with carded wool. Expect the finished sausage to round out somewhat in the felting. Photo the author.

105. *Villi Series: Three Modules* by Karen Van Derpool, 9″ x 9″ x 2½″ (22.9 x 22.9 x 6.4 cm). Solid felt sausage or cylindrical shapes are caught into the surface of flat felt tiles, creating an interesting play of forms and positive and negative spaces. Photo John Wesley.

I haven't tried to felt anything in a mold on a large scale and I don't believe anyone else has either. Since the wet wool is compressed so much when pressed into a solid shape, large-scale forms present not only technical problems, but create extremely heavy structures that are also wasteful of wool.

Solid felt—balls, sausages, thick flat rectangles, and the like—can be sliced, cut into, and, if hard enough, even carved. This presents yet another range of design possibilities. Pat Boutin Wald suggests, for example, slicing a small solid ball as one would slice a tomato, creating a series of round flat disks (buttons) of gradated sizes. A series of identical disks could be made, similarly, by slicing a long felt sausage. The cross-section surface of the disks can also be very interesting visually: depending on the fibers and colors stuffed into the mold, a variety of color and texture patterns may be revealed when the ball is sliced [118]. The usefulness and sturdiness of the disks depend largely on the density of the original ball; they must be very solid to be sliced satisfactorily. Use very short fiber (cut long-staple wool into short pieces) and stuff the form as tightly as possible. Slicing is best done with a quick, strong motion that produces a smooth cut. A slower, sawing motion will make a ragged uneven surface and will pull the wool out of its compact form. Pat Boutin Wald suggests using an electric knife, which works well with hard felt. Very sharp knives (Chinese-style cleavers are good) and skiving tools (long handled, Exacto-type knives used in bookbinding) also work well. A regular Exacto knife or razor blade is a little difficult to handle, because the blade is too small. A band saw should also work if it can be controlled on such a small object.

It would be difficult to literally carve handmade felt with hand tools (even if the felt were extremely hard and solid, it would not be as hard as wood or stone and could not be gouged or chipped), but it might be possible. As I pointed out in Chapter Three, extremely dense commercial felt is often shaped on a lathe. If you can make very hard felt and have access to a lathe, you might explore the possibilities of this technique. You might also consider carving commercially made sheet felt.

A related technique, also discussed earlier, is the stamping out of shapes. Stamping is done on a machine essentially similar to a large hole punch, with a custom-made die for each shape. You would probably have to enlist the help of people in industry to pursue this. You could have a special die made to order or you could rent factory time on an already existing die. To my knowledge, the possibilities of stamping and punching out felt shapes have not been explored to date by hand feltmakers, but exploration of this type might be worthwhile. A particular shape could be designed, for example, to be used as a module in a three dimensional construction or a flat collagelike tapestry. The shape could be stamped out hundreds or even thousands of times, and the modules arranged in any fashion—one on top of another, like a stack of pancakes, building out in any direction; in an overlapping grid; at right angles to one another; and so on. The shape itself could have an interesting mix of positive and negative space, and the modules could be stamped out of felts of different colors or varying shades of a single color, allowing color blending to be one of the key elements of the piece.

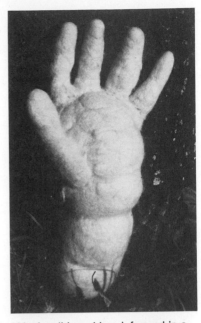

106. A solid wool hand, formed in a rubber glove and felted in a clothes dryer. Pinholes were punched in the rubber throughout the glove so water could escape. It was difficult to produce a well-proportioned hand and to keep the fingers attached to the palm. Photo the author.

107. When uncarded wool is stuffed into a mold, the felted ball may be uneven. In this experimental piece, the wool separated into three sections. Although difficult to control, this technique could be intentionally used for effects of this kind. Photo the author.

CHAPTER SIX

Working with Color

Felt is an ideal medium with which to explore color. Wool has a natural affinity for dyes and felt is a true showplace for rich dyed colors. Subtle color variations and nuances are literally trapped in place and no structural complexities compete with them visually.

Color effects may take quite different forms. The palette can be limited to natural colors—soft pastel shades that blend into one another—or vibrant, contrasting primary hues that nearly shout out from the felt surface. Color can penetrate the whole piece, lie just on the surface, or be confined to an internal layer.

THE NATURAL COLORS OF FIBERS

Many wonderful effects are possible when only the natural colors of the raw materials are employed. Even when wool is used exclusively, a wide range of whites, off-whites, browns, grays, and blacks can be combined. Dark areas might ripple through light areas, or vice versa, creating a marbled look [77]. Marbling is extremely effective in felt; the sense of fluidity is caught—trapped in time—as it is pressed in the fabric.

Layering and sandwiching are also effective with natural wools. Alternate layers of contrasting colors can be built up in the felt batt [108] or a sequence of shades can be built up on top of one another. The important design element here is usually the edge of the finished felt, where the layers (Barbara Setsu Pickett refers to them as "sedimentary planes") really show. The edges can be cut and positioned so they are exposed and highlighted in the finished felt [114, and Plate 8, Plate 14]. The layers of color beneath the surface are also visible when the felt is cut open [109, 110]. We are given an intimate look at the very structure of the material, as if the secrets of the felt were revealing themselves.

By adding other fibers to the wool felt, new colors and tonal qualities are created. A small quantity of camel hair, for example, will give the fabric a tawny color and a softer texture. Silk, being lustrous, catches and reflects light more than wool; thus, wool-silk felt has a special shine [84]. Rayon and certain synthetics can have the same effect: small touches of these materials add glimmering points of light to the felt. Dog hair, goat hair, and other animal and vegetable fibers all will change the color as well as the texture of the felt when mixed with the wool.

108. Color "sandwiches" are formed by alternating two colors or building up a sequence of colors in the felt batt. Photo Larry Beede.

FLEECE AND FELT DYEING

Essentially, there are two different times when dyeing can be done: before the material is felted (fleece dyeing) or after it is felted (felt dyeing). Both techniques are useful and each is appropriate for certain projects. Fleece dyeing (it should be understood that I am talking about dyeing the raw materials, which need not be entirely wool fleece) is generally most appropriate for shaded, gradated color effects where many tones will be blended in a single piece of felt, or for pieces where a variety of colors will be pressed into the top or layered surfaces. Because the raw fiber can mat easily and must be handled carefully, fleece dyeing is generally more time consuming and difficult to control than felt dyeing. Felt dyeing is simpler, but because the colors produced on any one piece of felt will probably be monochromatic, it will not on the whole produce the same kind of color as fleece dyeing. It is most appropriate for large, monochromatic felts or for smaller pieces that will be cut up and pieced together.

Note that after fleece dyeing, it is usually necessary to recard the fleece before forming it into a felt batt. This may be unnecessary if your fleece is thoroughly carded before dyeing. When the dyed fibers are dry, carefully pull them apart into the strips that will form the perpendicular layers of the batt. To assure that the surface of your finished felt will be even, you can recard only those strips that will comprise the top and bottom layers of the felt.

TYPES OF DYES

Many types of dyes can be used to color wool. Natural dyes can produce soft, lovely shades—these are often the most subtle colors—and felt is a medium in which they can be shown to good advantage. Feltmakers have complained, however, that fleece-dyed natural colors tend to fade or bleed out during the rough treatment of the felting process. Other dyes may be stronger, but if you are partial to working with natural dyes, try to minimize this problem by using strong rather than fugitive dyes with good lightfastness (ability to withstand exposure to light without fading); dyeing the fleece several shades darker than the color you are really aiming for (remember, the color will look much darker in the dyebath, before the fleece has been rinsed and dried); and rinsing the fiber thoroughly after dyeing, until the water runs absolutely clear.

Acid dyes are probably the most successful of the chemical dyes used with wool (natural dyeing actually involves chemicals, too, of course), for they have an affinity for all protein fibers (thus, they are also "attracted" to silk and other animal fibers: camel, dog, rabbit, et cetera). They are especially noted for their permanent, strong, vibrant colors—which can mean, of course, anything from brilliant primary colors to subtle, soft tints or shades. An acid dyebath generally includes an acid—usually acetic (of which vinegar is a dilute solution) or sulfuric—and a salt—Glauber's salt, or sodium sulfate, works best—both mixed in water before the fiber is added. The dyebath is heated. Brand names for acid dye include Ciba Kiton (probably the most popular), Ciba Nenzyl, Eriosin, Carbolan, Nylomine, Aljo, Craftool black label, Keco-Acid, Lissamine, and Kriegrocene.

Premetallized dyes, similar to acid dyes, also work well with wool. They can be thought of as a natural extension and later development of mordant dyes; their name is taken from the fact that the mordant, or metallic salt, is an actual part of the dye formula. Cibalan and Irgalan are brand names for these dyes.

The most recently developed dyes are fiber reactive. As their name implies, they actually react chemically with the fiber as no other dyes can. These may be successfully used with wool, but they are slightly harder on the fiber because the dyeing process involves alkaline materials. Some fiber-reactive dyes can be used in cold water and they are often used with batiks for this reason. Brand names for fiber-reactive dyes include Procion (Dylon, Fabdec, Fibrec, Hi-Dye, and Putnam Colorfast); Levafix; Cibacron; Procinyl; and Remazol.

Recently the safety of home dyeing with these dyes has been called into question. The dye powder can react with mucous membranes in the lungs and elsewhere to cause severe respiratory allergies. To minimize the danger from fiber-reactive or any other dyes, use gloves when dyeing or handling dye powder and wear a dust-filter mask to avoid inhaling the powder. Goggles will also protect the eyes from possible splashing of hot dye liquid. See Michael McCann's *Artist Beware* for further information on dye hazards.

Direct dyes (including Chlorantine, Durazol, Chlorazol, Keco-Direct, Craftool red label, Calcomine, Fezan, and Dick Blick); vat dyes (Cibanone, Inkodye, Caledon, Soledon, Durindone); and napthol dyes (Neutrogen, Rapidogen, GAF, American, Hoechst) are three other categories of dyestuffs available. These are of less interest to feltmakers as they are primarily intended for cellulosic fibers (cotton, linen, rayon, et cetera) rather than protein fibers. Disperse dyes (Dispersol, Duranol, Procinyl) are used on synthetic materials. Basic dyes (the original synthetic or aniline dyes) can be used on wool, but they are not very colorfast, so they are a poor choice for feltmaking. Brand names in this category are Synacril, Astrazon, Sevron, and Genacryl.

Do *not* use RIT, Tintex, or other dyes available in the supermarket, certainly not for fleece dyeing. Cushing and Putnam All-Purpose dyes are a little better, but they are also in the category of household (also called *union* or *mixture*) dyes. As Mary Ann Glantz pointed out in an article in the Summer 1971 issue of *Shuttle Spindle & Dyepot*:

These are mixtures of several classes of dyes: Direct dyes, Acid dyes, Basic dyes, and probably some Disperse dyes. . . . They also contain some acetic acid and a lot of salt, plus other chemicals. One of the reasons they fade so badly is that all of the dye does not have an affinity with the fiber you are dyeing, so that the dyes which are not correct for your particular fiber wash out or fade in the sun.

Clearly, these dyes will not stand up satisfactorily to the felting process.

DYEING PROCEDURES AND VARIATIONS

Excellent detailed instructions for dyeing with these various types of dyes can be found elsewhere (see the Bibliography) and commercial dyestuffs packaged for craft and household markets should also include instructions. Let me remind you, however, of general rules that should be kept in mind for all kinds of dyeing. These rules apply both to fleece and felt dyeing, though some may be more critical with the former.

First, the fiber (or already made felt) should be thoroughly clean and totally saturated with water (wetted out) before being submerged in the dyebath. Greasy or dirty wool will dye unevenly, as the cleaner parts will be more receptive to dye than others. Wet fiber, similarly, is most receptive to dye. If dry fiber is used, it will take longer to dye; if unevenly wet fiber is used, the wetter areas will dye more readily than the drier ones.

The fiber must be handled gently. Lay it in the dyebath with care; for best results, pack fleece loosely in a net bag for extra protection. Always put it in lukewarm water and raise the temperature of the dyebath *slowly*. The dye will penetrate more thoroughly and the fiber will be subjected to less shock. When the dyeing is complete, allow the fiber to cool to room temperature in the dyebath before it is removed and rinsed. Rinse in water the same temperature as the fiber; all rinse baths should be approximately the same temperature. Don't put loose fiber directly under running water. Rather, submerge it in a prepared rinse bath of clear water. Use as many baths as necessary to remove excess dye—the last rinse water should be completely clear.

If you want even dyeing, be especially careful to dye slowly and use a leveling agent in the dyebath. Glauber's salt is the most common and effective of these. It works by slowing down the bonding reaction between the fibers and the dye, thus allowing the color to spread more evenly. You can also weight the fiber down with a plate or some other flat heavy object, so it is completely submerged in the dye liquid. This prevents light streaks in areas of the fiber that might otherwise have been floating above the dye.

If you are interested in subtle color variations and blending, however, you may decide to *allow* the dyeing to be streaky and uneven. This will result in some fibers being slightly lighter or darker in tone than others. There are also other ways of increasing the number of shades that can be produced from a single dyebath. By simply taking a portion of the fiber out of the dye before the rest, for example, you produce two different shades of the same color. This can be done several times, producing a range of colors from light to dark. Similarly, some of the fiber can be treated with different mordants (setting agents, used primarily with natural dyes) or rinses (an acid rinse such as vinegar or an alkaline rinse such as ammonia can change a color radi-

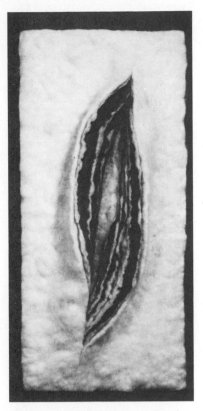

109. *Terra Madre* by Marleah Drexler MacDougal, 25″ x 11″ x 3″ (63.5 x 27.9 x 7.6 cm). A seemingly plain white felt is boldly slashed open, revealing multiple layers of color and texture beneath the surface. Courtesy the artist.

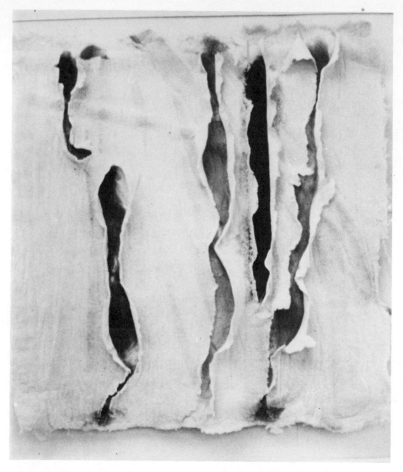

110. Beth Beede peels back the top layer of *Emergence*, 62″ x 58″ (157.4 x 147.4 cm), to reveal areas of vibrant primary colors below. Here the revelation is slower, the emergence more gradual, but it is immensely powerful. The large scale of the piece contributes to its power. Photo Larry Beede.

cally). Fiber can also be overdyed; that is, dyed first in one dyebath, rinsed thoroughly, and dyed in another bath of a different color. The two colors will visually blend together, creating the effect of a third color. Overdyeing works with most kinds of dyes, but it is generally not successful to overdye one class of dye over another—a fiber-reactive dye over an acid dye, for example.

Margaret Rhein notes that she sometimes dyes "ikat fashion." She binds off some areas of the wool with plastic so they resist the dye [Plate 2]. Resist dyeing can be done at any point in the dyeing process: the wool can be bound before being put in a dyebath at all; it can be taken out of the dyebath, bound, and put back in; it can be bound and put in a dyebath of another color, and so forth.

Graying and *blooming* dyebaths can also be used. A graying ("saddening") bath is a weak dye or mordant bath that will tone down color without actually changing it. When working with natural dyes, for example, a very small amount of ferrous sulfate (iron granules) mixed with water will gray the color. Coffee grounds or tea leaves, both of which contain tannic acid, also work this way. Tea leaves (wrapped securely in cheesecloth or some other porous bag) are often used, in fact, to give an "antique" look to white fabric. If you have commercially bleached wool batts or you want a felt that is not overly white, try this graying process even if no other dyeing is done. With chemical dyes, experiment with very weak solutions of tan, gray, or brown dye for graying effects.

A blooming or lightening dyebath, conversely, is one that will add a little more life to a color. A short simmer in a yellow dye, for example, can spark up a red, orange, or brown. A short time in a light grass green dyebath will lighten, though not substantially change, a very dark green. With natural dyes, a pinch of tin (stannous chloride) may help brighten any dyebath. All blooming baths must be used on darker colors; otherwise, the color may be changed rather than enlivened. Be sure to put sample bits of fiber in the lightening or graying baths first, so you won't be unhappily surprised by a change of color.

Graying baths and weak dyebaths of any color are also useful for visually unifying a wide variety of shades. If you have six entirely unrelated colors, for example, you can put them all in the same graying or weak dyebath, thereby giving them all a similar cast without actually changing their individual colors.

RESIST DYEING AND PRINTING ON FELT

I have already mentioned binding off certain areas of the fiber before dyeing so that a range of colors can be achieved. When tie dyeing is done on finished felt, the effect is usually soft and subtle, for the felt spreads the color somewhat and the boundary between tied and untied color areas is not sharp. Other kinds of resist dyeing, involving starchy pastes or waxes (batik), can also be attempted. These materials are applied to selected areas of the fabric, allowed to dry, and the fabric is then dyed in a cool bath. (A hot dyebath will melt the wax and break up the paste; for this reason, Procion type-M fiber-reactive dyes, which need not be heated, are recommended.) Dye will only be absorbed, of course, in the areas uncovered by resist materials. Pastes can be peeled or scraped off after dyeing; wax can be treated the same way, boiled out, dissolved in solvents, or ironed out. Because felt is so absorbent, it might be difficult to remove all of the resist material; it is also possible that some of the wool will be raised up off the surface as the resist comes off. These effects might even be desirable, however, and the problems should not be insurmountable. Experiments might well be worthwhile. Recipes and instructions for resist pastes are available in Esther Dendel's *African Fabric Crafts* or Thelma Newman's *Contemporary African Arts and Crafts*, and extensive batik instructions are in Joanifer Gibbs's *Batik Unlimited*, Dona Meilach's *Contemporary Batik & Tie-Dye*, or several other books listed in the bibliography.

Felt can also be used as the background material for printing and dye painting of various kinds. The nature of the felt will, of course, affect the image to some degree. A loose felt will produce a fuzzier edge than a tight felt, for example, and felt with a puckered surface will absorb the printing ink or dye in a somewhat uneven fashion. The effects can be very interesting and there is enormous design potential in this area.

Silkscreening on felt can be done in several ways. Screen stencils can be made from paper, lacquer or lacquer films, or a variety of photographic emulsions of photographic images. The printing itself can be done with prepared pigments or a number of different dyes. The difference between pigments and dyes is well explained by Richard Valentino and Phyllis Mufson in *Fabric Printing: Screen Method*.

Dyes and pigments are coloring agents. Used correctly they produce durable permanent colors, but they do it in different ways. The color quality is similar, but pigments are more resistant to fading and dyes tend to be more washfast. In pigments, the coloring agent is suspended in a plastic solution which surrounds and penetrates the fiber. Dyes, however, produce a chemical reaction that changes the molecular structure of the fiber.

Pigments store well, can be purchased ready mixed, and are applied as purchased. Dyes must be prepared at the time of dyeing. Screenprinting dyes also must be treated with a thickening agent so they become pastelike and, in most cases, they must be "fixed" to the fabric after dyeing, usually with steam and pressure.

Acid dyes, which work so well with wool, can be used effectively for textile printing. Beth Beede's hemlock branch [111], for example, was made by exposing the image onto a screen prepared with a direct photographic emulsion, Nazdar's Incasol, making, in effect, a photographic stencil with a positive image. The image was then printed on felt that had been rinsed in a strong vinegar solution and steam-ironed as smooth as possible. The dye itself was mixed with vinegar and a sodium alginate thickening agent (Keltex was used in this case, but sodium alginate is also sold under other brand names, such as Manutex or Lamitex). After the image was thoroughly dry, the piece was pressed again with a steam iron. Beede has done a number of prints this way and they have all stood up well to regular washing. Clear instructions for preparing direct emulsions and other types of photo-silkscreens and screening techniques are in Valentino and Mufson's book.

Until recently, fiber-reactive dyes were not as effective for printing on wool because the dyebath had to be heated. A promising new method has recently been developed, however, for the Procion M-type dyes. Simply stated, the dye is made into a paste, printed on the fabric, and allowed to set for 12 to 24 hours. The printed image develops at room temperature, with no heating or steaming. Finally, the fabric is washed. The colors achieved are said to be bright and strong. Detailed information about this type of printing is available in the Winter 1978 issue of the *Textile Artists Newsletter*.

It is interesting to note that printed felt rugs were popular in the 1930s for use under the dining-room table. Factory made, they were inexpensive and considered "expendable," so they were put in areas where they were likely to become stained and heavily worn. They were often used over other rugs or carpeting as well.

Images can also be made on felt by applying dye paste with a brush or airbrush. Woodblock and linoleum-block printing could also be experimented with. Again, felt will take dye or ink just as any other fabric, but because of its unique surface, it will yield unusual—and potentially exciting—results.

111. Detail of a photo-silkscreen print of a hemlock branch by Beth Beede. Acid dye was mixed with vinegar and a thickening agent; images printed this way hold up well to dry cleaning, even washing. Photo Larry Beede.

COLOR BLENDING IN FELTING

The possibilities presented by color blending are among the most interesting and unique aspects of feltmaking. When pigments (in paints, dyes, inks, et cetera) are mixed, new colors are created, but no traces of the original colors remain. In weaving, colors can be mixed in a visual sense only: blues and yellows crossing over and under one another, for example, can create the impression of green. In feltmaking, the visual blending can be carried even further. Individual *fibers* wind through one another in a haphazard fashion; the visually blended color is more irregular, more subtle, and more complex than in weaving. Even tiny specks of colored fiber can make a difference visually. Gayle Luchessa, in an interview with Gwen Stone in *Visual Dialog* (December 1976) remarked that, "White [felt] pieces were laminated with lint from my washing machine, producing subtle color effects reminiscent of pastels and very painterly in appearance."

There are many ways to approach color blending and any number of them can be used in combination. Fleece dyed in different dyebaths can be carded together in a single rolag or batt and, depending on the way the colors are positioned on the card (or carding machine), a sprinkling of a number of colors or a single overall new color will be created. If black and white fleece are spread in completely even amounts on the card, for example, the carded rolag will appear gray. If the black fleece is centered on the card, surrounded by white fleece, the rolag will have a black stripe in the middle [112]. (The edges of the stripe will not be straight and hard, of course, and when felted they will be even softer. Even if the black area is very dark, there will be some gray where the black wool meets the white.) The stripe can be used in turn to create designs. If each rolag had a dark stripe in its center, for example, the finished felt would have a more or less regular repeat of such stripes. Stripes could be laid in a gradating color sequence; they could be placed in different areas of the rolags to form a random pattern in the felt; streaks or blotches of color could be used instead of stripes. The possibilities go on and on.

Solid-color rolags or batts may also be positioned next to each other in the felt batt. This, too, might be done in any number of ways. Subtle color changes could be made by gradually shifting from dark red to light red to pink, for instance, or from black to gray to white [113]. Four different colors could be used in the four quadrants of the batt. Color could be concentrated in one area, such as the frame or the center of the batt. Rolags and carded batts made in one single color can, of course, also be torn or cut up into smaller pieces and repositioned in relation to

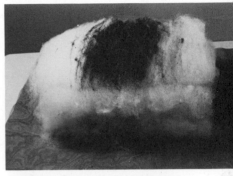

112. The top layer of this felt batt was made by centering an area of black fleece between areas of white fleece on a drum carder. During carding, a few black fibers shifted toward the edges, so the borderline between light and dark areas is not distinct. This effect will be even more exaggerated after felting. Photo Larry Beede.

113. Shades from light to dark can be gradated within one batt (the dark rolag at right is added for photographic contrast only), or between several batts or pieces of felt in a single finished piece. Photo Larry Beede.

other colors; a checkerboard might be made in this way. Finished felts of varying colors can also be blended by being juxtaposed against one another in appliqué, collage, or a variety of constructed forms [Plate 3].

I have already discussed building up layers of different shades of color in the felt batt. Layering can also be done with a variety of colors, and multicolored layers open up all kinds of artistic possibilities. Several artists have worked with felt strips. Kristy Higby, for example, cut layered felt into long narrow pieces and rolled and sewed them together with their edges exposed in *Sweeter Fare* [114]. The colored layers wrapping around one another are truly sensuous and evocative. Patricia Williams also worked with the edges of colored strips in her series of *Layered Surfaces* [115]. Her felt is much softer and fluffier than Higby's and the colors blend into one another more gently.

Felt strips can also be *re*felted with interesting results. They tend to become much rounder and harder during a second felting; as tubular shapes, they offer still more design possibilities. Margaret Rhein has worked with this idea. In one of her pieces, tubular strips are attached to one another side by side, in a vertical plane, much as the tubular pipes of a pipe organ are. In another piece, strips of soft felt were attached to one another at regular crosspoints, forming a grid. They were worked into one another with continued fulling.

Layering need not be done on a flat plane; intriguing effects can be achieved by building up colors around or inside molds. Circular color patterns can be formed, for example, by wrapping a series of colors around one another, stuffing the circular batt into a stocking, and felting it into a solid ball. When the ball is cut open, swirling colors are revealed [118]. Random spots of color can, of course, be worked into any shape; the layering need not be regular.

COLOR INLAY: "FELT PAINTING"
Inlaid color designs were briefly mentioned in Chapter Two in conjunction with historical felt rugs. To reiterate, predyed wool, unspun, lightly spun, or lightly felted, is laid out in a pattern either directly underneath or directly on top of the wool batt be-

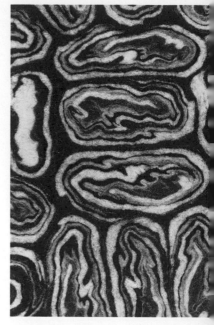

114. Sliced rolls of multicolored felt are stitched together in Kristy L. Higby's *Sweeter Fare,* 15″ x 23″ (38.1 x 58.4 cm), a detail of which appears here. See also [Plate 8]. Photo Rick Gast.

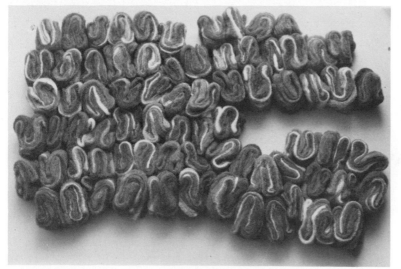

115. *Layered Surface 2* by Patricia Williams, 15″ x 22″ x 2″ (38.1 x 55.9 x 5.1 cm). Like Higby, Williams also explores the effect of layered color, but here the felt is much softer and looser. This is one of a series of pieces in which layered felt strips are arranged in different formations. Courtesy the artist.

116. Laura Basanta used layers of soft felt in a range of purples for *Purple Felt*, 18″ x 25″ (45.7 x 63.5 cm). Photo Bill Gilliss.

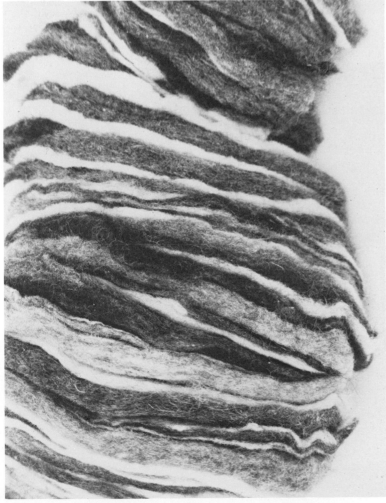

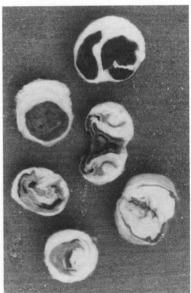

117. (Left) Detail of *Caterpillar* by Deborah McMahon. Slices of felt with multilayered and multicolored edges are strung together into a long form, which highlights the edge even further. Courtesy the artist.

118. (Above) A group of felt balls sliced open to reveal hidden swirls of color. Photo the author.

fore felting [119, 120]. It felts along with the batt and becomes an integral part of the finished felt. Color inlay is an apt and descriptive term, for the color and design are literally laid on and pressed in the felt. The design is usually laid on only one surface, but designs *can* be placed both above and below the same batt, creating inlaid patterns on both sides of the felt. Rugs used to cover the floors in Turkoman yurts are always made this way.

Before the felting actually begins, there is room for a great deal of experimentation with this technique. Line and color can be added, subtracted, shifted—it's like laying out collage materials and moving them around to the proper position before glueing them down. The process is sometimes referred to as "felt painting." Many artists remark on the "aerial quality" and the "watercolor feeling" of inlaid designs.

When unspun fleece is used for the inlay, it will, as might be expected, produce designs with very soft, fuzzy edges. When the

119. On this small sample of the color inlay technique, the design was first laid out in unspun colored wool on a bamboo screen; here the first layer of rolags is being laid over it. This is closest to the traditional Central Asian technique. Photo Larry Beede.

120. A playful design in wool pencil roving was laid on top of a four-layer felt batt in this experimental piece by the author. The batt is basted in an envelope of nylon netting. When the design is laid on the surface of a batt that will be worked by hand, start the hardening process by felting on the opposite side: there will be less danger of the design shifting. Photo the author.

121. *Ocean* by Deone Tremblay, 36″ x 54″ (91.4 x 137.2 cm). A large piece with inlaid designs, with a free, flowing sense of movement. See also [Plate 13]. Courtesy the artist.

design calls for a clearly defined line or outline, use lightly spun yarn; this will hold its shape fairly well yet still felt in thoroughly. When defined areas of color with relatively strong edges are desired, it's usually a good idea to use lightly felted wool. Like spun wool, this will hold its shape but still felt into the surface of the new felt. Cut edges on lightly felted wool will soften when they are refelted in this way.

Plan your design with the felting action in mind. Don't use images with fine detail, sharp angles, or very straight lines. Baste the wool to the backing material carefully, across the whole surface of the batt, and work with the batt in a rolled position so no pressure will be applied directly on the design during the felting process. Always allow for a certain amount of shrinkage, slippage, and distortion. Try not to work with inlay too close to the edge of the piece because it will tend to work its way over; the edges are the area of the felt most difficult to control precisely. Don't full the piece in the dryer, for the intensity of the heat and tumbling may distort the design too much. Above all, choose designs that take full advantage of the qualities of the felt and work *well* with the inevitable slippage. Deborah Kaufman, who has truly mastered the color inlay technique, remarks that she "tries to select images that are strong enough to not only be recognizable even though distorted, but can take the distortion with a 'sense of humor.' . . . The changes imposed on lines and forms in the felt process emphasize this."

POSTSCRIPT: OTHER COLOR IDEAS

We have been talking about standard dyeing and coloring practices, but there is room for a great deal of further imaginative experimentation when it comes to felt and color. People have been trying such unusual techniques as blowing dye powder directly on the surface of a soft felt and then fulling it further, working the color in; brushing liquid dye on the surface—actually painting with it—or pouring it on; or placing certain natural dyestuffs, such as onionskins and flowers, right in the layered batt and felting them in. Cheryl Patton McManamy even worked

122. (Above) *Plaid Shirt* by Deborah Kaufman, 36″ x 26″ (91.4 x 66 cm), is made in the color inlay technique. Kaufman's clothing pieces are, in her words, "conceived of as spirit catchers, portraits without people." Photo Roger B. Smith.

123. (Right) Detail of *Plaid Shirt* by Deborah Kaufman. Photo Roger B. Smith.

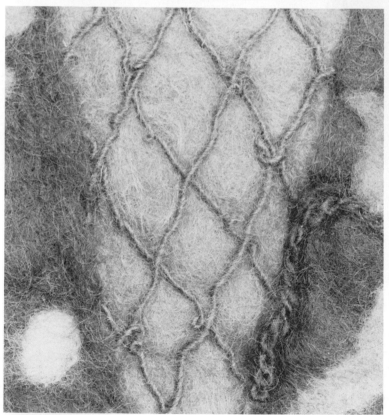

124. (Above) *Housecoat* by Deborah Kaufman, 58″ x 36″ (147.3 x 91.4 cm). Photo Roger B. Smith.

125. (Right) Detail of *Housecoat* by Deborah Kaufman. Photo Roger B. Smith.

with face powder to "stain" her felt, creating a "musty, almost mildewed" effect. If you use a substantial amount of nonprotein fiber in your felt, you might also take a hint from industry: when commercial felt is made from a combination of wool and rayon (a cellulosic fiber), both direct and acid dyes are used in successive dyebaths.

Play with subtle varieties of natural white fleece; soft pastels and intensive rich hues; and with marbling, mottling, streaking, and spotting. Try *anything* in your experimental pieces. There is no need to be afraid of failure, because unsuccessful felt designs and color can be covered with other layers of fleece and refelted, cut up and used as design elements in new pieces, or redyed completely to a new, darker shade.

126. *Sue's Landscape* by Beth Beede, 24″ x 36″ (61 x 91.4 cm). The soft quality of this inlaid design is reminiscent of a watercolor. The piece is made in a variety of earth tones. Photo Larry Beede.

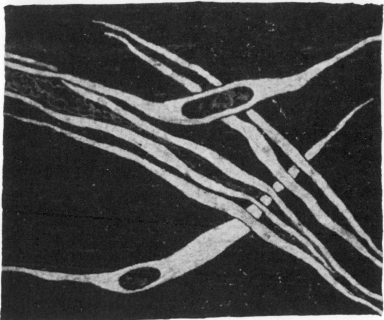

127. *Smooth Cells* by Lynn Reiter Weinberg, 41″ x 45″ (104 x 114.4 cm). This is not an inlaid design; the foreground pieces are appliquéd on the background. The shapes are fluid, but the edges are crisp and clearly defined. Weinberg often uses biological imagery in her work. Courtesy the artist.

CHAPTER SEVEN

Explorations

Up to this point I have discussed the principles of basic feltmaking, forming and shaping with felt, and color. These are the building blocks, so to speak, of feltmaking as an artistic medium. They can be used to make a variety of artistic statements. This chapter goes a bit further than the building blocks to explore auxiliary ideas in more detail. It focuses on ways of combining basic techniques, exploiting the properties of felt, working on a large scale and mechanizing the felting process, and using felt for clothing. Suggestions are also made for new areas of exploration. I hope this chapter will help bring the rest of the book together and serve as a compendium of possibilities and an impetus for new creative endeavor.

EXPLORING THE FELT SURFACE

I have, of course, already discussed the felt surface; one cannot talk about feltmaking without doing so. I've mentioned that the surface can appear hard or soft, that it can be brushed up or ironed down, that it can be highly textured or relatively smooth, and so on. We will now explore these issues further.

The density and quality of the felt surface will have a great deal to do with the overall feeling of any felt form. It seems simplistic to say that soft felt will appear soft and hard felt will appear hard, but these are actual qualities that will strongly affect a piece; they should be controlled and used consciously to convey an overall idea. Compare, for example, the soft felt in Ruth Geneslaw's *Embossed Form* [145], Pam Bell's *Fall Duck* [148], or Kristy Higby's *Sheep Shells* [128] with the harder felt in Nancy Algrim's pieces [84–87], Sherold Barr's *Moonlite Currents* [92], or Joan Livingstone's *Sentinel I* [132]. The integrity of any of these would be severely weakened if the quality of the felt were altered. Be sure to consider the qualities you want in your felt: the light, buoyant, almost vulnerable feeling evoked by very soft felt; the firm, compact, almost impenetrable feeling of very hard felt; or something in between.

When making felt and striving for specific surface textures, there are a few things to keep in mind. First, remember that a felt batt made up of a few thick layers of batts or rolags will generally produce a softer, less dense felt than a batt made up of a greater number of thin layers. This will be true even if the height of the finished batt is equal in both cases.

The type of fiber will definitely affect the felt surface. When certain wools have been heavily fulled, they tend to felt with a

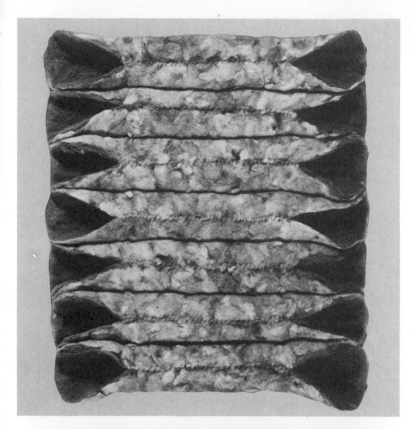

128. *Sheep Shells* by Kristy L. Higby, 18″ x 16″ (45.7 x 40.6 cm). Hollow forms of soft, pastel-color felt are stacked and sewn together. Note the interplay between the inside and outside of the shells and how effectively the marbled color works on the light surfaces. Photo Rick Gast.

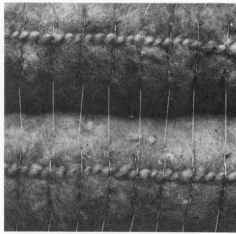

129. (Left) *Abacus* by Kristy L. Higby, 19″ x 16″ (48.3 x 40.6 cm).

130. (Above) Detail of *Abacus* by Kristy L. Higby.

131. Detail of *Mapped Felt* by Joan Livingstone. Livingstone, one of the pioneers in contemporary feltmaking, has impressive control over the medium. In their entirety, her pieces are powerful and strong; in every detail, their rich textured surfaces are suggestive and evocative. Photo George Crary. Courtesy The Hadler-Rodriguez Galleries, New York.

132. *Sentinel II* by Joan Livingstone, 77″ x 58″ x 20″ (196 x 147 x 51 cm). The scale of this free-standing piece is indeed imposing, as is appropriate for a sentinel. Three wooden triangular, structural elements are embedded in the felt and yarns and color are laid in the surface. The piece is reminiscent of landscapes, cave paintings, and skeletal forms, but also has an immediacy and intensity that is compelling. See also [Plate 16]. Photo George Crary. Courtesy The Hadler-Rodriguez Galleries, New York.

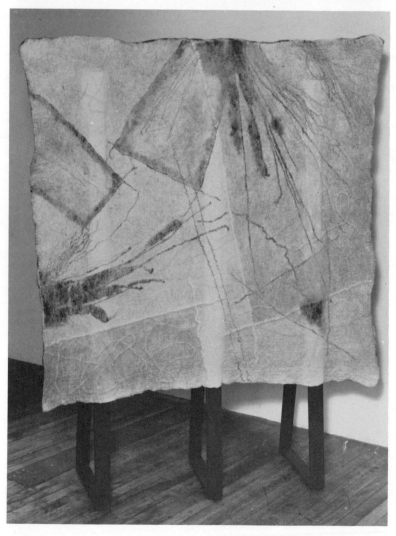

122

pebbly, lunar-surface look [90, 131]. Generally, long-fibered fleece produces this effect, but there are too many variables and too many exceptions to make such a statement categorically. Combinations of short and long wools, which felt at different rates, also result in puckered effects in many cases. These puckered surfaces can be enormously engaging and evocative, as can be seen in Georgia Stegmeier's *Stone Wall* [100] or Joan Livingstone's *Mapped Felt* [131]. Felt made of short, heavily crimped fleece like Merino *usually* has a smoother surface, as no fibers are winding their way through a large portion of the tangled mass and thereby buckling in different places. Felt made in mechanical hardening machines, where there is a regular, repeated action, is also usually smoother-surfaced than handmade felt, which is subjected to less pressure and uneven agitation. (Mechanical hardening machines made for home use are discussed later in this chapter.)

Different areas of any piece can, certainly, make use of different felt qualities. Whether the piece is composed of a number of separate felt sections or made as one unit, it may have both hard and soft areas. The initial felt batt may be built up in some spots more than others, certain sections may be subjected to extra fulling, or some areas may be pulled slightly apart at the soft-felt state. Lightly felted pieces can also be added to heavily felted pieces.

One of the most wonderful qualities of felt is its ability to trap things in itself. All kinds of fibers and objects can be embedded. As I mentioned in Chapter Five, one way to do this is to catch the materials between layers of the wool batt, thereby creating raised areas on the surface of the felt. Many artists refer to this technique as "embossing." Embedding materials so their raised silhouette is visible can be a little tricky, for they sometimes seem to get lost in the layers of the wool and show up poorly. My experiments have led me to conclude that relatively thick embedding materials—at least 3/8 of an inch thick—are easiest to work with. They should be placed just below the top layer in the batt and covered with just enough fiber to felt them in. It's a good idea to baste directly around the embedded materials when preparing the batt, "locking" them in place. Fulling should be done until the piece is quite hard. If the embedded materials do seem lost after fulling, consider stitching around them to bring them into greater relief; use thread the same color as the felt so the stitching is as invisible as possible.

Materials trapped between layers of thin, soft felt may not stand up from the surface, but they may be visible when light shines from behind. The felt, with all its air spaces, is more translucent than the trapped material and the contrast can be intriguing. Patterns and images may actually be invisible, then, until the piece is placed under certain lighting conditions.

Rather than laying fibers or other objects between layers of the wool batt and hardening them from the beginning of the feltmaking process, you can also put them into the piece part way through the process. Barbara Setsu Pickett suggests, for example, cutting into soft felt and inserting a heavy thread. After further hardening and fulling, the thread makes a sharp, straight line in the felt. (A thread laid between layers of the batt, on the other hand, would be more difficult to control—more likely to slip—and difficult to form in this kind of sharp line.) Ropes,

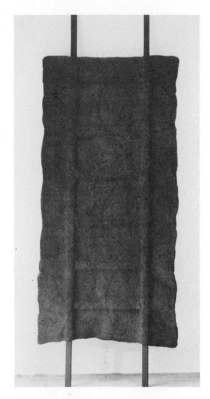

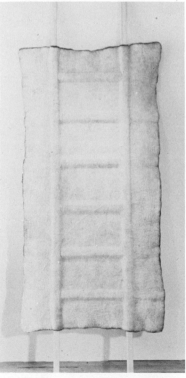

133. *Night Ladder I and II* by Joan Livingstone, felt and wood, 99″ high (259 cm). Photo George Crary. Courtesy The Hadler-Rodriguez Galleries, New York.

123

134. *Drifters and Runes* is indicative of the evolution of Joan Livingstone's work, each element about 48″ high (122 cm). In this recent (1979) piece, the structures are becoming increasingly architectural, more consciously defining the overall space as well as the interrelationships of the individual parts. The thick, dense felt that gives the piece so much of its force is characteristic of Livingstone's work. Wood, plaster, and paint are used here with the skeletal forms. Photo Frank Hamilton.

135. *Memory Shroud* by Anne Dushanko-Dobek, 72″ high (182.9 cm). It is designed to hang in front of a wall so shadows are cast. Laces and other materials were embedded below the top layer of the felt batt. Courtesy the artist.

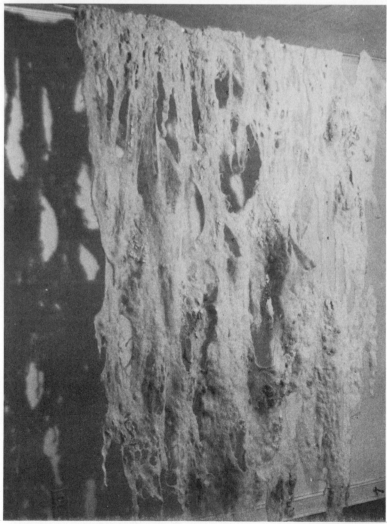

sticks, and other materials could be used instead of thread.

Materials can also be caught in the felt in such a way that they move in and out of the surface—partly above and partly below it [136, 138–140]. This is a wonderful way to play with felt; layers and planes reveal themselves, "secrets" are partially revealed yet still tantalizing and mysterious. A sense of the elasticity and vitality of the individual wool fibers is also brought into play, giving the piece a dynamic quality, a sense of elements springing into life.

One way of achieving this in-and-out effect was discussed in Chapter Five: resists can be used to block off some areas of a material during the felting process. A resist is not necessary in every case, however. In Joanne Mattera's *Felted Fiber Drawing* [139], for example, the yarn was simply laid on the surface and covered in some areas with a thin layer of fleece. The depth from which the trapped material emerges can be controlled by the judicious placement of fiber on the top surface—higher in some areas than others.

Wool and other fibers, pieces of felt, fabrics, and other materials can also lie *on* the felt surface [141]. (Actually, there will have to be an area of interface between the background felt and the surface material; one cannot technically be completely above the other, but I am primarily talking about visual effect.) It is easiest to work these materials onto the felt surface when the felt has been worked slightly (at the soft-felt stage). At this point, there are still enough loose fibers to really catch the materials, yet the fabric is formed enough to hold its shape. Be sure to brush the base felt to bring up its nap before laying down the surface materials.

Several feltmakers have used roving, top, or loosely spun yarn to create a powerful surface-on-a-surface. In Pat Spark's *White Weaving* [137], for example, the top surface is like an enlarged, three-dimensional picture of a weaving. (Spark has taken this idea even further; see below.) Roger Thomason, similarly, uses roving and top for strong, snakelike forms on many of his pieces [142]. These large-scale surface forms, highly evocative and sensuous, tend to provoke strong reactions from people seeing them for the first time.

Felt that has been cut or molded into small shapes can easily and effectively be attached to another felt surface. This is usually done, again, at the soft-felt stage, but Barbara Setsu Pickett also recommends cutting shapes out of semihardened felt and putting them directly over felt batts (under the backing fabric or screen). Margaret Rhein, who has done a good deal of experimentation with balls and other molded forms, has made several pieces where highly textured sliced shapes are felted to other felts [143]. She has also felted solid balls to felt strips, and to one another. In *Villi Series: Three Modules* [105], Karen Van Derpool felted cylindrical felt forms to flat "tiles." In all of these pieces there are intriguing interactions between flat and molded surface, as well as interplay between light and shadow, positive and negative space.

Lightly spun wool, wool roving, or crocheted, knitted, or netted constructions can also be felted directly into three-dimensional forms without a background surface. If roving is simply put in a bath of boiling water (it can be a dyebath) and stirred frequently, it will tend to felt into a tight rope. When roving is

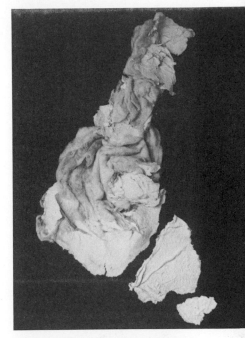

136. *It's Just a Small Separation* by Cheryl Patton McManamy, 60½″ x 24½″ x 6″ (153.7 x 62.2 x 15.2 cm). Handmade felt and paper are worked into one another in this large piece, which highlights the relationship between the two materials. Photo Rex McManamy.

137. *White Weaving* by Pat Spark, 13½″ x 14½″ (34.3 x 36.8 cm). Wool top was used in this piece to form a specific image. The shapes that evolve with this technique are naturally organic and fluid. Spark finds it exhilarating to be forced to "work with nature" in the felting process. Courtesy the artist.

138. Detail of *Memory Vault #4*, one of 10 elements, by Anne Dushanko-Dobek. White gloves are felted into and with wool and surrounded with sisal. A variety of found objects are caught among the fibers in these 10 "vaults": feathers, barbed wire, a delicate white shoe. They ask us to remember and confront our own associations and memories. Courtesy the artist.

139. Detail of *Felted Fiber Drawing* by Joanne Mattera, one of a series investigating fiber as a linear element. Silk threads twist their way in and out of the wool and camel-hair felt. Almost magically, we see them beneath a thin layer of wool as they seem to float within the piece. Courtesy the artist.

140. Detail of an experimental felt made by a student of Joanne Mattera. A two-ply yarn is felted to a layer below the surface of the piece, but is visible in many areas where the top layer has torn away. The elastic, tensile quality of the wool is evident where the felt is drawing apart. Photo Joanne Mattera.

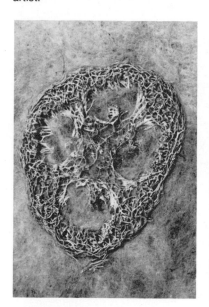

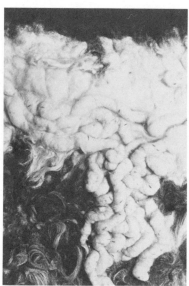

141. Sliced sections of a loofa sponge were felted into natural wool in this experimental piece by Beth Beede. Note how completely the wool has become an integral part of the sponge, particularly in the center. Photo Larry Beede.

142. Detail of *Cloud Series #2* by Roger K. Thomason, wool felt, wool roving, raw fleece, yarn. The roving has been used on this piece for dense, rhythmical surface relief. Photo Jack Eby.

143. Detail of *Colored Rain in a Blue Pool* by Margaret Rhein. Multicolored felt balls are sliced with an electric knife and arranged in different color sequences on a carded batt background. "Having created single building elements," Rhein states, "I then play and interplay these." Photo Marty Mulligan.

used as a construction element, as it was in Pat Spark's *Non-Woven Fabric* [146], and then put in a hot bath, it felts into an extremely strong form. Anne Dushanko-Dobek created a "large wool net with no distracting knots, a great deal of strength, and little or no potential for breaking or stretching under its own weight" by netting loosely formed wool on top of a large sheet, pinning it randomly in place, covering it with a second sheet, basting it together, and felting it in the washing machine.

Another way to approach highly sculptured surfaces is to work with techniques that allow unfelted wool staple or the felt itself to come out, or rise from, the surface. The raised dots on Ruth Geneslaw's *Embossed Form* [145] are made by poking holes in the muslin backing cloth and allowing some fibers to migrate through during the felting process. A similar idea was worked out by Hillary Farkas. Inspired by the hairdresser's technique of frosting hair—pulling selected strands through a cloth and dyeing the tips of those and no others—Farkas developed a way to make felt with long, fleecelike pile [Steps 1–6]. Locks of long lustrous fleece are placed on top of a felt batt and partially pulled through holes in a muslin cloth placed above them. The parts of the locks that lie beneath the muslin are felted in with the regular felt batt; the part that has been pulled through the holes is prevented from felting at all. The result is similar to a sheepskin: a solid felted "pelt" almost completely covered by a long wool staple.

Lynn Sullivan, an Australian fiber artist, tried a very similar technique, which she refers to as "feltmaking by hooking." She stretched fine wire mesh over a frame, positioned the frame across two sawhorses, and placed carded fleece on top of it. She then laid underneath the frame and drew fleece through the mesh with a hook. The whole piece was subjected to some hardening action. This produced a very soft but strong felt with little shrinkage and no distortion (the mesh kept the shape stretched out). Sullivan vows she'll never do it again, however, because it was too time consuming.

Sullivan and a few other contemporary feltmakers have also experimented with felting a whole, uncarded fleece. Sullivan claims this technique works well when the fleece has a very high (60 plus) count with many surface locks. (*Count* is a figure that

144. *Subsoil* by Lynda Lowe Oren, 63″ x 26″ (160 x 66 cm). A fascinating piece that speaks of subterranean secrets and movement. Oren recently received a grant to visit Leningrad to study the Scythian felts housed in The Hermitage. Courtesy the artist.

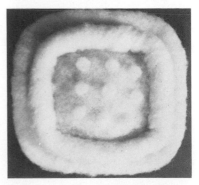

145. (Above) *Embossed Form* by Ruth Geneslaw, 6″ square (15.2 cm). This small piece is encased in Plexiglas, which both protects and sets it off. The soft quality of the felt is in sharp contrast to the smooth, hard plastic. Courtesy the artist.

146. (Left) *Non-Woven Fabric* by Pat Spark, 20″ x 24″ (50.8 x 61 cm). Although the strength and dimensional stability of this piece result from felting, the individual elements are, indeed, woven through one another. Courtesy the artist.

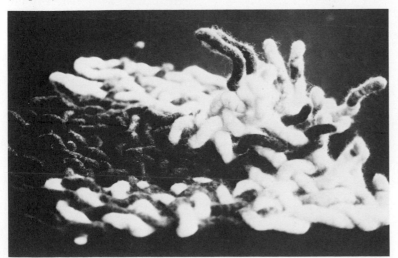

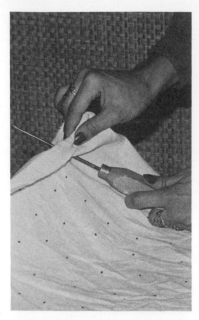 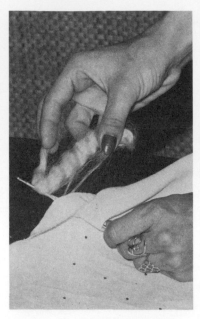 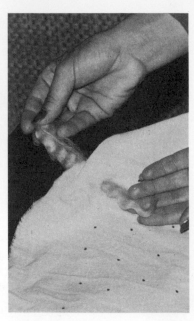

Step 1. Mark a piece of prewashed muslin or an old sheet with dots at regular intervals, about 1½″ to 2″ (3.8 to 5 cm) apart (the exact distance will vary depending on the desired density of the pile). Use an ice pick or another sharp implement to pierce the fabric and make a hole at each dot. Photo Stan Farkas.

Step 2. Using a crochet hook, draw a long, clean, curly wool lock about halfway through from the back to the front of the fabric in each hole. Keep all cut ends on one side, all uncut tips on the other. The fleece used here is from a New Zealand Border Leicester sheep. Photo Stan Farkas.

Step 3. Leave *at least* 1″ (2.5 cm) of the lock on the back side of the fabric so there will be enough wool to be caught into the regular felt batt. Photo Stan Farkas.

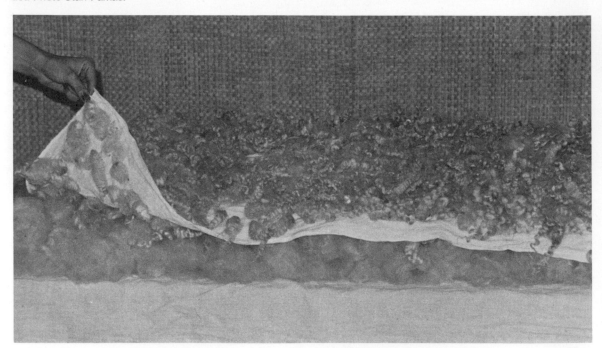

Step 4. Prepare the felt batt and lay it on top of muslin or another backing cloth. If the entire piece will be covered with the wool locks, it is possible to use a thick bed of well-teased fleece, without carding or layering. Cover this with the muslin that holds the locks, leaving the cut ends on the batt. Cover this layer with another piece of muslin and sew the whole sandwich (two outer layers of muslin, two wool layers, and one central muslin layer) together. Photo Stan Farkas.

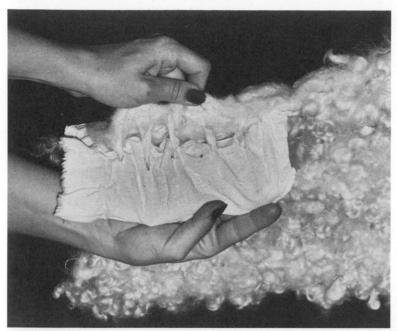

Step 5. (Left) Felt the piece by hand, working only on the side *opposite* the loose locks. It can be put in the dryer for continued fulling; this will pull the locks together well, but will probably shrink the piece a great deal (as much as 75%: beware!). Remove the stitches and the outer pieces of muslin and carefully work the central muslin layer out. This will be somewhat difficult, for it will have the resistance of the felt all around it. Cut into the muslin a little bit at a time as you pull the locks out. The cut end of the fleece should be thoroughly embedded in the bottom felt layer. Photo Stan Farkas.

Step 6. (Below) The finished "fleece" can be used as any other felt might be. Here it has been folded into a tubular shape in preparation for further work. Photo Stan Farkas.

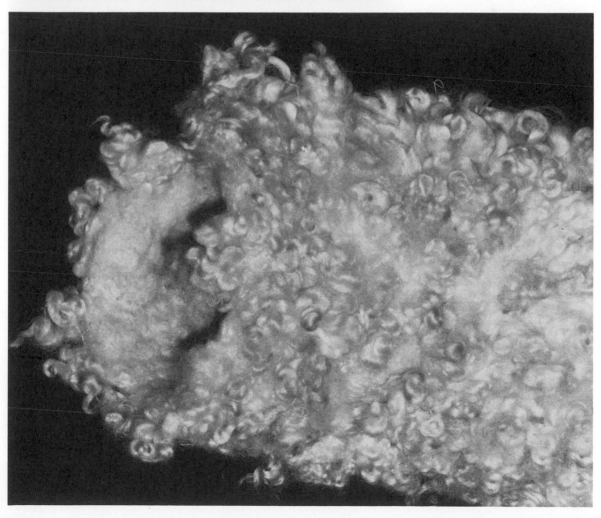

identifies the fineness or coarseness of the wool. Technically, it refers to the number of hanks of yarn, each 560 yards long, that can be spun from one pound of wool top. Since finer wool will produce thinner yarn, it will have a high count—about 60–70—while coarse wool will have a low count—in the range of 20–30.) Dawn MacNutt, a Canadian, likes to use this technique when the fleece is "faulty," especially if the cut side is already badly matted. She finds it works best with Leicester or Lincoln wool. Sullivan felts by hand, but MacNutt felts the fleece in the washing machine. The technique of felting an entire fleece, you may recall, was also used in Tibet, where it was often used for clothing. The shaggy, uneven, pockmarked surface presented an interesting texture. (If you're thinking of following suit, however, back it with some other fabric for it is likely to be unevenly felted and not very strong.)

Wool's ability to catch on itself can be used in yet another way that will transform the felt surface—will make it, in fact, part of another surface. Molly Fowler has worked with felt as a background behind open warps in woven tapestries [147]. She makes soft felt and suspends it about three-quarters of an inch behind a warp stretched on an upright frame. She weaves normally with a wool weft and, as she works, the felt attaches itself to the weaving. Subtle changes in color and tone in the felt show through unwoven areas in the tapestry, drawing the whole piece together visually. Fowler had tried a number of other background materials (corduroy and others), but was always dissatisfied until she tried felt. Finally pleased with the visual impact, she was doubly delighted when she realized the felt had become an integral part of the tapestry. In her more recent pieces, she has also taken to adding felt figures to the front of the warp. Felt may also be attached to crocheted, knitted, laced, or netted yarns in a similar fashion.

FELT AS FABRIC

Felt is, of course, a fabric. As such, it can be used as any other fabric: it can be cut up, stitched, appliquéd, painted or printed on, rubberized, made into clothing, and so on. Its unique characteristics—a highly absorbent surface, relatively stiff draping properties, and a great deal of body and strength—should be kept in mind and worked with to fullest advantage at all times.

Although it is difficult to achieve designs with sharp edges—because the color will penetrate the fibers and spread unevenly, just as the fibers themselves form no regular or linear pattern—this tendency toward distortion can be used to advantage. It can even be taken further after a printed design is firmly set, by pulling the felt apart slightly or raising the surface nap.

The absorbent surface will also drink up a number of other substances, all of which will affect the overall visual and tactile qualities of the felt. Lynn Mauser-Bain has applied Rhoplex and latex to felt, and next plans to pour hot, black tar over "pristine white" felts. Felt dipped in shellac, lacquer, or high-gloss paint also becomes stiff and unyielding—totally transformed. There is a long-standing precedent for this, of course, in the hatting industry (see Chapters Two and Three). It is interesting to note that environmental conditions affect the felt's requirements for a rubberizing or stiffening agent. As John Thomson, the 19th-century hatter, put it:

> There is no department in the hatting trade of more importance than that of stiffening, as the kind, quality and quantity of the stiff must be regulated according to the country in which the hats are to be worn. England, for instance, where there is so much moisture in the atmosphere, requires a much harder stiff than we do in America.

I am not recommending any stiffening or plasticizing materials as actual finishes, or as ways of making too-soft felt harder. With these materials, the original quality of the felt will probably be entirely changed. (Molly Fowler reports, in fact, that she tried using Hyplar and Permastarch to strengthen her felts, but neither worked satisfactorily.) It is when the transformation becomes the *point* of the piece that these materials might be effectively used.

Everything that can be done with commercial "novelty" or dimestore-variety felt can be effectively reinterpreted with handmade felt; more interesting textures and colors will make the usual unusual. There are a great many "feltcraft" books available and, as an exercise, you might look through them and try to visualize the way the pieces would look with handmade felt.

Felt makes an excellent background for stitchery, appliqué, and other applied designs [148, 149]. It is also effective as a foreground material: think of those wonderful Scythian "mosaics" described in Chapter Two. Because of its excellent insulating and soundproofing properties, it is useful as a covering for architectural structures (the yurt, the lean-to) or as a wall covering. In winter, Beth Beede covers a wall of her Connecticut farmhouse with individually designed, interconnecting felt panels. Interchangeable rectangles (or pie-shaped wedges or whatever) of dense felt might also be used for a rug, even a wall-to-wall carpet. Dense felt has enough weight and body to stand without support and also lends itself to innumerable free-standing sculptural possibilities.

Perhaps because of the contrast between them, felt works well with baskets and basketry materials. It can weave in and out of semirigid stanchions; it can be enclosed in them; it can enclose them. As a wrapping material, soft felt is sensuous and enveloping; it evokes feelings of warmth and security.

When felt is cut or torn into strips, it can function as an element, rather than as a fabric. It can be woven, plaited, braided,

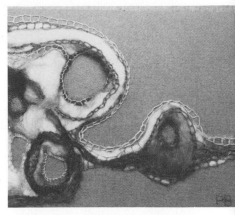

148. Soft felt is effectively used with stitchery to convey a feeling of movement and vitality in *Fall Duck* by Pam Bell, 10″ x 12″ (25.4 x 30.5 cm). The stitchery and background are also wool. Photo Steven Vedro.

149. Embroidery on the felt surface has been traditional in India for years. This detail of a *Numdah* rug illustrates the way embroidery gently molds the felt surface. Photo the author.

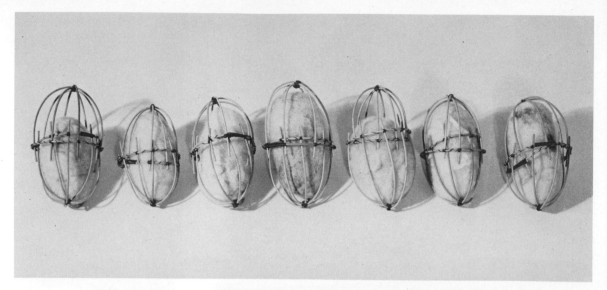

150. (Top) *Solution I* by Laura S. Basanta, each module approximately 4″–5″ long (10.2–12.7 cm). Oval felt forms are enclosed in "shells" made of cane and thread. The felt becomes somehow precious, guarded patiently by another rigid-yet-flexible material. Collection Georgetown College, Georgetown, Kentucky. Photo Bill Gilliss.

151. (Above) *Felt Bundles* by Roger K. Thomason, straw rope, wool and alpaca top, fleece, wool yarn, each approximately 14″ x 3″ (35.6 x 7.6 cm). The contrast between materials is one reason why this piece is interesting. The wool felt is soft and enveloping, the straw harder, more prickly. Photo Jack Eby.

152. (Right) Detail of *The Audience* by Arlene Mylenek, vegetable-dyed wool and yarn. "I basically work with the creation of a surface and the change of that surface, as pieces break away or . . . fall apart." Courtesy Detroit Felt Collective.

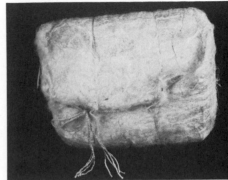

looped, or crocheted, and made into new forms. The strips can be used as they are, or refelted into one piece. Thus, when a multiple-element construction like a plaited basket is subjected to water and hardening action, it can become, in a sense, a single-element construction.

FELT CLOTHING

As we have seen earlier, felt is a wonderful material for certain types of clothing. It insulates well, sheds water and ice, and does not deteriorate with exposure to the elements. As a fabric it is usually relatively heavy and has a great deal of body, but will still drape to a certain extent. These properties have made it most useful for outer garments and it has been used to cover everything from head to foot.

I have described some of the traditional felt garments of Central Asia, the Far East, and Scandinavia, and traditional felt hats in both East and West. It should be noted, too, that once felt-making was mechanized, felt clothing was also made by commercial industrial establishments. John Thomson mentions felt leggings, mittens, caps, and gaiters, all made by his company in 1868. (He boasted that, because of their strength and traction, one who wore his felt gaiters could "walk upon the slippery pavement with comfort and full confidence.")

There was a resurgence of interest in felt clothing after World War II, when commercial manufacturers searched for peacetime civilian markets and uses for felt products and processes developed during the war. Many readers will remember the ubiquitous felt skirts of the 1950s [156]. Dresses, coats, slippers, vests, boleros, and hats were also made of felt. These were monochromatic, smooth-surfaced felts with little textural interest (though they were sometimes printed with large-scale designs) and their popularity was short-lived.

A new interest in felt clothing is emerging, but today's clothing is entirely different. It is made from handmade felt that, in contrast to the felt of the '50s, is thick and full-bodied and rich in texture and tone. Contemporary feltmakers have the freedom to draw from many stylistic and decorative traditions, without being limited by them, and can integrate a great many techniques

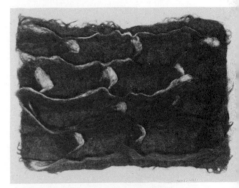

in one piece. Traditional clothing patterns are transformed by this "new" material; entirely new forms, suggested by the material itself, are emerging. Many of the new felt outergarments carry associations with the earth, the forest, and the trees; others evoke warm, womblike places.

I feel instructions for making clothing, as such, would be limiting and counterproductive to creative thinking. They would in any case be incomplete. I do, however, wish to pass on some of the things that feltmakers who have worked with garments have found.

As might be expected, one of the first concerns is the strength of the garment and the kind of movement and strain it can withstand. Exposing a flat or mobile piece of felt to the elements is one thing, but exposing a cut, tailored, felt garment—with constant stress in certain areas—is quite another. Many traditional "ethnic" felt garments (for example, the Turkish kepenek, the Tibetan or Chinese poncho or cape) sidestep this problem entirely by being suspended over the body. Boxy, rectangular, or circular shapes are easier to work with and eliminate areas of stress. Many contemporary felt artists have almost instinctively found the same solution. They have turned to felt capes, ponchos, and vests, which use the shoulders as a frame and minimize the problems of underarm and side seams. Lynn Barnett-

156. (Above) Felt garments were quite popular during the 1950s. This girl's jumper, somewhat stiff in *hand* or feel, has a brushed surface. Note that both cut and seamed edges were used successfully. Courtesy Merrimack Valley Textile Museum, North Andover, Massachusetts.

157. (Left) *Wilderness Poncho* by Betsey Klompus. Positive and negative spaces give a feeling of primal, wild forms. The piece is lined throughout. Courtesy the artist.

158. (Opposite page, top) Back view of a crocheted, woolen, hiplength jacket by Denise Welch-May, with overlapping felt "scales" in the central section. Welch-May turned to felting as a way to build up large color areas in her work. She has gone on to new directions with the medium, but even with this early piece she believes felt is what "made it work." Photo Rich Starr.

159. (Right) Contemporary coat of handmade felt by Nancy A. Bowser. The textural quality of a coat made of handmade felt is considerably different than a commercial one. Dark wool was added to the top of the felt batt for the tonal variation on the surface. Photo the artist and John La Rose.

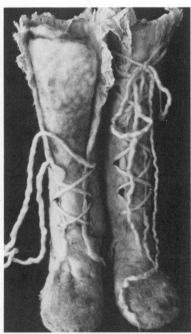

160. (Above) Meg Cantor's *Boots for Trampling through Grandma's Roses*, 26″ high (66 cm), were molded in several pieces and stitched together. Red thorns are used as hooks, the delicate lace lining is glued on with epoxy, the laces are felted roving. These boots have a rather ephemeral feeling and are not made to be worn. Courtesy the artist.

161. Jacket by Susan E. Nestel, felted with wool, mohair, and flax. Textural detail can be as much the focus in a garment as in any other piece of felt. The artist was especially pleased with the way the flax felted: "It took on the appearance of wool—looked crimpy on a larger scale." Photo Tom Steele.

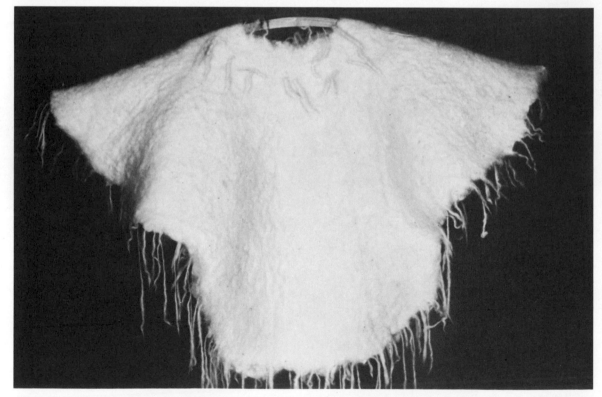

162. Poncho by Beth Beede and Judy Heywood. By being suspended on the shoulders, this garment, like Klompus's *Wilderness Poncho*, solves the problem of wear and strain in certain areas of the felt. Traditional felt garments in Central Asia were usually made according to the same principle. This poncho is also lined, to reduce friction against clothing. Photo Larry Beede.

Westfall found another way of addressing this problem: she made front and back pieces for a vest and attached them to flexible crocheted panels at the shoulders and sides.

Some artists also use interlayers in their batts when the felt is going to be used for clothing. Cheesecloth, nylon "bridal" netting, or even horsehair is laid in about the center of the batt to help produce a stronger, more solid (and usually stiffer) felt, which is less likely to be pulled out of shape. Lining the felt or quilting it to a backing fabric can have the same effect.

In Sweden, boots, socks, and mittens are often made with the *flatsom* technique. Roughly translated, this means "braided seam." Loosely spun wool yarn is threaded through a heavy needle and the entire surface of a shaped wool batt is stitched through with herringbone stitches [163]. The stitches become completely embedded when the piece is felted. They keep the molded form of the piece intact and, because they serve as a supporting structure, less fulling is needed to make a very strong felt. The process itself, however, is very time consuming and the stitches are prominently visible—as a kind of latticework—when the piece is finished.

Making felt of the appropriate size and quality for specific garments is one of the other problems you may encounter. The exact amount of shrinkage is difficult to predict and the overall feeling of the finished felt may not be exactly what you had anticipated. Always make samples of the felt first, calculate approximate shrinkage, and allow *at least* that much extra felt when making an actual pattern. Better yet, allow even more for unexpected shrinkage or other problems. If necessary, change your original design so the garment really *works* with felt—it should be appropriate to its texture, weight, and overall feeling.

There are ways of dealing with felt clothing that is not exactly the right size. In Sweden, felt socks were adjusted for individual people in several ways. If they had become too tight in the felting process or were too small for a particular person, they were cut up the front and laced. (Rivets can be punched into the felt for the laces, much as they would be in leather.) If the boots were too wide, they were cut, wrapped so one cut end overlapped the other, and buttoned. Decorative accents on these Swedish socks and boots included fur, crochet, and embroidery.

Remember, too, that felt itself can serve as an accent for other kinds of garments. Pat Boutin Wald's felt buttons could be applied to other fabrics. Felt strips could be used as trimming, in much the same way as an inkle band might be. Fringe could be made from very thin felt strips, or from yarn or roving felted in hot water into solid round forms. The accent can be as practical and mundane as a felt reinforcement patch on the elbows of a sweater, or as frivolous and outrageous as molded felt breasts or plaited felt breastplates.

WORKING ON A LARGE SCALE

Many people who have mastered feltmaking on the small scale described in Chapter Four still feel overwhelmed or intimidated by the prospect of working on a very large scale. As Melonie Rufty put it, "It takes an enormous amount of strength and energy to harden the felt. . . . I usually have to work on a smaller scale and combine the pieces."

There is no question that if you are going to make a single,

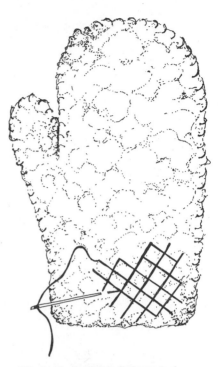

163. In the Swedish *flatsom* technique, used for making very strong felt, a herringbone stitch is applied all over the surface of the felt batt before hardening. The stitches become thoroughly felted in the fabric and add dimensional stability to it. Illustration Jeanne Freer.

164. Mukluks by Beth Beede. Beede, who homesteaded in Alaska for many years, used a traditional Eskimo pattern and added crochet trim in woolen yarn. Photo Larry Beede.

large piece of felt, a great deal of work and effort must go into it. Lynda Lowe Oren, whose felt pieces are often as large as 8 by 7 feet, works up to 20 hours hardening a single piece. She enlists help when she can, but more often than not she works alone. Oren uses a method similar to the "foot" method we described earlier. She works on a floor with a drainage hole, or outside, and uses a garden hose for water and some pressure. She places her batts in fiberglass screening and, like the Central Asians, primarily uses a rolling-unrolling action for hardening and fulling. As she puts it, "it is essential to participate body and soul, using feet, knees, forearms, and hands to work the felt." Lynn Sullivan found it took four days to felt a large piece by the rolling method. Her piece shrank dramatically—from nine by six feet to five by four feet—but this was due in part to the wool, a high-count Merino fleece.

The best way to make a large piece of felt is to work with a group of people. Nomadic feltmakers always did this, as did feltmakers in traditional Central Asian workshops. (It is sometimes made today by just one person, only because the craft is dying rapidly.) Children love to work on this kind of project [168] and though they may lose interest before too long, even 15 minutes of hardening with an eager group of helpers will make a difference. Try to get them to sing songs and work rhythmically in unison.

Adults can also be encouraged to felt together, giving rise to a wonderful social occasion. Invite friends to contribute their labor to an artistic endeavor, much as was done in the traditional quilting bee. At the "milling frolics" or "waulking bees" that were traditional for fulling handwoven Scotch tartans, blankets, and other cloth, there were standard songs and foods. Other traditions of these occasions might also be adopted. Traditionally,

165. (Left) Hat by Denise Welch-May. Felt is mixed with crochet and a sheepskin ruff; the materials complement each other well. Photo Rich Starr.

166. (Above) Wolf hair is incorporated into *Loki*, a mask by Beth Beede, 24" high (61 cm). The basic form was molded over a felt ball. This mask has also been used in performances. Photo Larry Beede.

167. (Above) *Free Standing Construction* by Katarina Weslien, 48″ × 36″ × 60″ (122 × 91.4 × 152.4 cm). Here structure has become self supporting by the use of larger inlaid dowels. Photo Harriet Hartigan.

168. (Left) Children helping Deone Tremblay felt *Ocean.* The piece was 96″ × 72″ (244 × 183 cm) before felting, 56″ × 40″ (142 × 101.5 cm) after felting. Working in a driveway can be ideal, for a garden hose can be used to keep the felt wet and the water will easily drain into the ground. Courtesy the artist.

for example, the work went on until the fabric had shrunk to a particular, predetermined size; different groups or teams alternated with one another—when one group tired, the other could take over—so it was possible to go on for many hours. The actual fulling was done around a long slatted table, like an overgrown washboard with slits, which allowed excess water to drain out. Contemporary group felting can be done the same way, or it can be done along the same lines as a grape-stomping: the batt is placed flat on the ground and participants walk over it with their bare feet.

MECHANIZING THE FELTING PROCESS

One other way to deal with the problems of felting on a large scale is to consider doing part of the process mechanically. This can mean anything from "pressing" the felt with a steam roller to building an actual hardening machine or convincing a commercial felt company to let you use or rent theirs.

Beth Beede has been able to work with both of the latter two alternatives. After approaching a number of felt manufacturers, she found one small plant where the workers were intrigued with her ideas and anxious to see how they would work. After regular working hours, they helped her put large batts in their hardener. In doing so, they found themselves learning more about the felt-making process, for they had never thought about the possibilities of embedding other objects and materials, laying in color, and so forth. The hardening was extremely fast and easy to do and all of the pieces felted successfully.

The experiments in the mill were exciting, but not sufficient; Beede was anxious to work at her own pace and not have to fit into spare hours in a commercial schedule. She and her husband Larry searched out early patents and plans for hardening machines and came up with one they could adapt and build themselves. The moist batt is placed between two heavy wooden plates; the bottom one is in a fixed position, the top one is free to oscillate. When the machine is turned on (it runs by an old fuel-pump motor or a hand crank), the top plate moves back and forth over the batt, working it with constant pressure. The working surface of this particular machine is about four feet square and it cost about 500 dollars in materials (excluding labor). A small, handturned version with a working surface about one foot square cost 55 dollars. Larry Beede has taken out a patent on the model, but is willing to sell the plans to others who would like to make one. (See Appendix for address.) He reminds people who might like to design machines of their own that there are a few things to keep in mind. The materials have to be durable, since they will be subjected to a great deal of vibration and water. For the same reason, all joints have to be tightly secured with screws and braces. The top plate has to be very heavy, but there must be a way to lift it easily. Lastly, there has to be allowance for drainage at the bottom.

Although this has been referred to as a hardening machine, it actually felts a piece completely; no further fulling is necessary for a strong felt. It is a pleasure to work with the machine and anyone planning to do a great deal of large-scale feltwork might seriously contemplate making one like it.

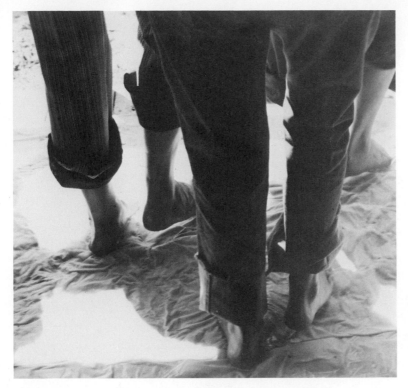

169. Members of a felting workshop at Brookfield Craft Center, Connecticut, work a large batt with their feet. Later, the hardened batt was taken inside and worked with a kneading motion, to the accompaniment of spirited singing and chanting. Photo the author.

AREAS STILL TO BE EXPLORED

Throughout the book, I have tried to point out aspects of felt-making that offer relatively untapped design potential. These include using quilting-type stitches as "drawing" materials, working with cut and stamped felt shapes, molding felt in unusual forms (all discussed in Chapter Five), and applying hardening, plasticizing, or rubberizing agents to transform the felt (Chapter Seven). In addition, areas of possible exploration in feltmaking, untouched to date by contemporary artists, were pointed out in 1974 by Marcia Chamberlain and Candace Crockett in their book, *Beyond Weaving*. At the time, they noted that many of the properties of felt that make it so valuable to industry—its ability to absorb water, sound, and vibration; its insulating and wicking qualities; and its ability to polish and seal—had been untapped by hand feltmakers. Essentially, this is still true, although the increasing use of felt in clothing and Beth Beede's felt wall indicate that its insulating properties, at least, are beginning to be exploited. Perhaps someone will emerge in the near future who will have the imaginative vision to put some of the other possibilities to work. A sculptor might use carved or molded felt in a large-scale piece, for example, where mechanical action or running water are involved. I hope this book provides enough background information and seed ideas to give these visionaries the groundwork for further exploration.

A Guide
to Wool

Note that actual grade count and staple length figures vary somewhat from source to source.

Breed	Average Staple Length & Classification	Average Fleece Weight	Grade or Count	Comments
Cheviot	4″ Medium	4–5 lb.	50–56	Semiluster, strong fiber.
Columbia	3½–5″ Medium crossbreed	15–20 lb.	50–60	Cross between Rambouillet and Lincoln.
Corriedale	6–8″ Medium crossbreed	10–12 lb.	50–60	Long, silky fiber. Bred from Leicester and Lincoln.
Cotswold	7–12″ Long	12–13 lb.	36–48	White curly fleece, inclined to mat.
Dorset	Down 2–3″ Horn 3–4″ Medium	5–7 lb.	48–56	Very white, strong close fleece, excellent for felt.
Hampshire	2–3″ Medium	5–6 lb.	48–60	Brown or black heads, noses, feet, legs. Short staple. Some black fleece may show up in white fleece.
Jacob	3–6″ Medium	4–6 lb.	44–56	Brown and white patches, quality variable. White usually softer than brown.
Leicester	7–9″ 12–14″ Long	11–13 lb.	to 48	Long staple, silky high-luster fleece. Wide crimp; makes coarse felt with much air —can see many of the individual fibers. Good to crochet into, make "pile" felt.
Lincoln	8–12″ 12–16″ Long	11–14 lb.	36–46	Similar to Leicester.
Merino	2–4″ Fine	9 lb. or more	65–100 (many different grades)	Creamy color, soft hand, high crimp. Felts easily, with high shrinkage; thus, difficult to control.

Breed	Average Staple Length & Classification	Average Fleece Weight	Grade or Count	Comments
Orkney	1½–3″	2½–5 lb.	50–56	Scottish. Various colors: red, fawn, brown, gray, white.
Oxford	3–6″ Medium crossbreed	8–10 lb.	46–50	Tendency to shed. Cross between Hampshire, Shropshire, Cotswold. Soft and easy to handle.
Rambouillet	2¼–3″ Fine	15–20 lb.	62–70	Developed from Merino. Slightly coarser but still fine. Felts quickly.
Romeldale	Long	10–14 lb.	58–60	Cross between Romney and Rambouillet; combines characteristics of both.
Romney	6–7″ Long	8½–10 lb.	40–48	Similar to Leicester. Favored by many feltmakers.
Rough Fell	8″ Long	5 lb.	32–36	Coarse, long staple with little crimp.
Shetland	4″ Medium	2–3 lb.	56–60	Various colors (similar to Orkney), with white wool softest.
Shropshire	3½–4½″ Medium	6–8 lb.	48–56	Fine, dense wool. Some black may be in white wool (see Hampshire).
Southdown	1–2½″ Fine–Medium	6 lb.	50–60	Very white, short, well-crimped fleece.
Suffolk	2–3″ Medium crossbreed	5½–7 lb.	48–58	Soft handle, light, airy fleece. Some black may be in white wool (see Hampshire).
Targhee	3″ Medium crossbreed		58–60	High-quality wool.

Supplies and Resources

American Felt Manufacturers
Association
National Textile Association
211 Congress Street
Boston, Massachusetts 02110
*Most felt manufacturers belong to
this organization. Use them as a
clearinghouse for information on
industrial/commercial establishments and procedures.*

Arachne Fiber Arts, Inc.
217 West San Francisco Street
Santa Fe, New Mexico 87501
*Fleece, roving, hand cards, Pro-
cion dyes.*

C. Bailey
15 Dutton Street
Bankstown
NSW 2200, Australia
Australian fleece and other wools.

Larry Beede
705 Middle Turnpike
Mansfield, Depot, CT 06251
Plans for hardening machine.

Cerulean Blue
P.O. Box 5126
1314 NE 43 Street
Seattle, Washington 98105
*Dyes of all kinds, textile-printing
supplies, airbrush equipment.*

D.Y.E. Textile Resources
3763 Durango Avenue
Los Angeles, California 90034
*Dyes of all kinds, textile-printing
supplies.*

The Fiber Studio
Foster Hill Road
Henniker, New Hampshire 03242
*Fleece, roving, mohair, alpaca,
camel, yak, and other fibers.*

Forte Fibers
P.O. Box 818
Palisade, Colorado 81526
*Wool, goat hair, camel, mohair,
cashmere, and other fibers.*

Patrick Green
15459-84th Avenue
Surrey, British Columbia
Canada V3S 2N3
Hand cards, felting brush.

Greentree Ranch Wools
The Countryside Weaver
163 North Carter Lake Road
Loveland, Colorado 80537
*Wool and fleece of all kinds,
hand cards, drum carder, other
fibers.*

Harrisville Designs
Harrisville, New Hampshire 03450
*Wool, cashmere, camel, mohair,
and a variety of other fibers.*

Hedgehog Equipment
Wheatcroft, Itchingfield
Horsham, Sussex, England
*English fleece, drum carder, card
clothing.*

The Mannings
East Berlin, Pennsylvania 17316
*Wool, roving, and a variety of
other fibers, hand cards, drum
carder.*

Romni Wools and Fibres
3779 West Tenth Avenue
Vancouver, British Columbia
Canada V6R 2G5
*Drum carder, fleece, llama, mo-
hair, camel, silk, and other novelty fibers.*

St. Peter Woolen Mill
101 West Broadway
St. Peter, Minnesota 56082
*Virgin wool batts in varying sizes,
custom carding (raw wool or old
"recyclable" wool).*

Something Special
5400 Park Lane Road
East Lansing, Michigan 48823
Mark IV drum carder.

The Spinning Wheel Factory
1666 Steeles Avenue West
Milton, Ontario
Canada L9T 2X8
*Mark IV drum carder, hand
cards.*

The Spinster
34 Hamilton Avenue
Sloatsburg, New York 10974
*Fleece, novelty fibers, and hand
cards.*

TALAS
Division Technical Library Service
130 Fifth Avenue
New York, New York 10011
Methyl cellulose and wheat-paste glues, and other archival materials.

Textile Artists Supply
(formerly Straw Into Gold)
5533 College Avenue
Oakland, California 94618
Dyes, natural dyestuffs and mordants, wool, and a wide variety of other animal and vegetable fibers, hand cards.

Wausau Woolen Company
408 South Fourth Street
Wausau, Wisconsin 54401
Virgin wool batts, commercially carded into single large pieces, each one to five pounds. Will card raw wool into batts and recard old woolen batts.

The Wool Bureau
Division International
Wool Secretariat
Technical Services Center
225 Crossways Park Drive
Woodbury, New York 11797
Technical information on wool and the wool industry in this country.

Check also display and classified advertisements in the following magazines:

American Craft
(formerly *Craft Horizons*)
44 West 53rd Street
New York, New York 10019

Fiberarts
50 College Street
Asheville, North Carolina 28801

Interweave (and *Spin-off*)
306 Washington Avenue
Loveland, Colorado 80537

Shuttle Spindle & Dyepot
65 La Salle Ròad
P.O. Box 7-374
West Hartford, Connecticut 06107

Weaving and Fiber News
(formerly *Weaver's Newsletter*)
P.O. Box 259
Homer, New York 13077

Glossary

Page numbers following entries refer to the place in the text where the term is first discussed or defined most extensively.

Bark Cloth (Beaten Bark Cloth): Matted fabric made from thoroughly beaten strips of bark. The fibers mesh together under pressure and the action of a resinous, viscous substance. Also called *Tapa Cloth*. (pp. 16–18)

Batt: An orderly mass of wool or other fiber. Wool peeled off a drum carder is a *wool batt*; loosened or carded wool arranged several inches high, usually in perpendicular layers, is a *felt batt*. (p. 8)

Body (Hat Body): A hollow, conical felt form; a working or preliminary form of a hat. (p. 43)

Carding: The process of opening up snags, loosening, and aligning wool or other fibers; a type of combing. (pp. 45, 57) See also *Carding Bow, Carding Machine, Hand Cards*.

Carding Bow: A large, violin-bow-like instrument used to align wool or fur fibers. When the bow is plucked by a skilled craftsman, the vibration of the bowstring causes currents of air to move the fiber. (pp. 30–31, 41–42)

Carding Machine: A device made of two or more rollers, each covered with fine wire teeth that turn against one another to card wool. (pp. 45, 57)

Carrotting: The process of treating fur fibers with a chemical solution to make them felt. The chemicals swell the fibers and their scales. (p. 41)

A carrotting formula used in 1868, according to John Thomson, consisted of "32 parts quicksilver [mercury] dissolved in 500 parts of aqua fortis ["strong water," or nitric acid], diluted with one-half to two-thirds bulk of water." Another formula used perchloride of mercury and white arsenic. The carrotting liquid was brushed on the upper part of the hairs. The usual fur mixture in the early American hatting industry was two parts carrotted fur to one part uncarrotted fur.

Contemporary carrotting formulas make use of acidulated hydrogen peroxide and nitric acid; cheap commercial hair felts (for example, cattle hair) used in polishing are sometimes treated with lime.

Cone: The first form of a hat *Body*. (p. 43)

Crimp: 1. The kinks or springlike curls of an individual wool fiber. (p. 9) 2. The kinking tendency of wool. (p. 9)

Cross-Lapping: Layering rolags or batts in a perpendicular fashion in the felt batt. (pp. 45, 63)

Directional Fiber Effect (D.F.E.): The one-way, rootward movement of wool fibers when they are subjected to the conditions of heat, moisture, and pressure. Because the fibers can *only* move in this way, they become irreversibly entangled or felted. (p. 9)

Embed: Trap materials between layers of the felt batt. (pp. 94–96, 123–125)

Emboss: Embed materials in such a way that they form a raised area or design on the surface of the felt. (p. 123)

Felt: 1. A pressed, matted fabric formed by the interlocking of wool and certain other fibers, made with no spinning, weaving, or knitting. (p. 8) 2. The process of making felt fabric.

Fleece: The already shorn wool of a sheep. The term refers to an entire fleece or to a mass of raw wool fibers. (pp. 53, 55)

Full, Fulling: The intense shrinking and interlocking of wool fibers through the action of moisture, pressure, and usually heat, occurring after they have been either felted together (hardened) or woven or knitted into a fabric. The latter is also called *Milling*. (pp. 8, 15)

Fuller's Earth: A powdery clay made of finely ground aluminum silicate, which absorbs dirt, grease, and impurities from finished fabrics and leaves them with a soft sheen. (p. 16)

Fur Felt: Felt made entirely from the short, fine fur fibers of such animals as beaver, nutria, or rabbit. Fur usually requires chemical preparation, or *Carrotting*, before felting. (pp. 40–41)

Hand Cards: A pair of wooden brushes, covered with fine wire bristles or teeth, used to card wool. (p. 57)

Harden, Hardening: The process of felting wool (and/or other fibers) to the point where it has formed a solid mass that will no longer come apart with gentle pressure. (p. 8)

Hard Felt: Felt that has been fulled and is dense and unpliable. (p. 69)

Inlaid Color, Inlaid Designs: Patterns made in felt by colored designs of unspun, loosely spun, or lightly felted wool laid on the backing material or wool batt. The design felts along with the rest of the wool. (pp. 31, 114–117)

Milling: See *Fulling.*

Needle-Woven (Needle-Punched, Needle-Loomed) Fabric: Feltlike fabric (usually synthetic) formed by the mechanical action of hundreds of barbed hooks or needles passing through a fiber batt. Indoor-outdoor carpet is often made this way. (pp. 18–19)

Noil: The very short wool fibers that lie close to the back of the sheep; too short for spinning, they are used in commercial hat and feltmaking. (pp. 40, 55)

Nonwoven Fabric: A synthetic fabric made by chemical or thermoplastic adhesion, or mechanical action; *Needlewoven Fabrics* are examples. (pp. 18–19)

Paper: Thin sheets made by beating or shredding cellulosic fibers, such as linen, cotton, bark, or wood, into a pulp, which is then mixed with water, formed on a sievelike screen, and pressed to remove excess water. (p. 18)

Resist: A material, such as cloth or paper, inserted between two layers of wool to keep them from felting together. (pp. 76–77)

Retting: The process of soaking a fibrous plant, such as flax, so as to loosen the fiber from the woody tissue. (p. 18)

Rolag: The fiber roll made from fleece prepared on *Hand Cards*; in Swedish, literally "rolled air." The smoothed-out fiber is rolled up the width of the card. (p. 57)

Roll Felt: Felt made commercially as yardage, in a long continuous roll. (p. 44)

Roving: Commercially prepared, combed, unspun, or very lightly spun fibers arranged in a parallel fashion in long strips. (p. 55)

Sheet Felt (Formed Felt): Extremely hard felt formed by hand in small sheets, usually one yard square. (p. 47)

Shocking: Subjecting wool fiber to extremes of very hot and very cold temperatures. (p. 66)

Soft Felt: Just-hardened felt; felt that has meshed together enough to form a solid mass, but can still be manipulated. (p. 69)

Stepping: A method of making felt with foot pressure. Usually, the pressure is applied by putting all one's weight on one leg (with knee bent), and using it to work the rolled batt. (pp. 71–72)

Stiffening: A starch, resin, or other agent that stiffens a material. (p. 43) An 18th-century American "stiff" involved two "boiling pots": one composed of "beer grounds" and vinegar, the other of a decoction of horse-chestnut leaves or other glue dissolved in water. The beer grounds were applied to the inside of the hat, and the stiffening glue was spread on it. As Mary Elizabeth McClellan tells us, it was "prevented, by the coating of the beer grounds, from soaking through to the face of the hat where it would hamper an even finish."

The "American stiff" in use during the late 19th century, according to John Thomson, was 20 pounds of orange shellac dissolved in 5 gallons of cold alcohol. Today, it is customary to use a mixture of shellac, mastic, turpentine, and tartar.

Tapa Cloth: See *Bark Cloth.*

Top: Commercially combed fiber prepared in long strips for spinning. (p. 55)

Wheel Felt: A very hard *Sheet*-type felt built up in round wheels. Used especially for polishing bobs and buffing wheels. (p. 47)

Bibliography

The letters following each reference are a key to the subjects covered by the work cited.

A. general historical and ethnographic information
B. feltmaking instructions
C. the felt industry
D. hatmaking
E. contemporary feltmaking
F. barkcloth, paper, and related techniques
G. technical information on dyeing, printing, wool, et cetera.

Agren, Katarina. *Tovning*. Forlaget, Sweden: I.C.A., Gamlia Museum, 1976. In Swedish. A, B, D.

Andrews, Peter A. and Andrews, Mugul. "The Turkmen Tent," in *The Turcoman of Iran,* ed. Mary E. Burkett and J. Allgrove. Kendall, England: The Abbot Hall Art Gallery, 1971. A.

Andrews, Peter A. "The White House of Khurasan: The Felt Tents of the Iranian Yomut and Goklen," *Iran* (Journal of the British Institute of Persian Studies), vol. 11 (1973). A.

Ballou, Maturin Murray. *Pictorial Drawing Room Companion*, vol. 9, no. 21 (1855). A.

Becker, William. "Designing with Felt," in *Machine Design.* Cleveland: Penton Publishing Company, 1969.

Bhavnani, Enakshi. "A Journey to Little Tibet," *National Geographic,* May 1951.

Burkett, Mary E. "Felt," in *The Turcoman of Iran,* ed. Mary E. Burkett and J. Allgrove. Kendall, England: The Abbot Hall Art Gallery, 1971. A.

Chamberlain, Marilyn and Crockett, Candace. *Beyond Weaving.* New York: Watson-Guptill Publications, 1974. E.

Clarke, W. *An Introduction to Textile Printing: A Practical Manual for Use in Laboratories, Colleges and Schools of Art.* New York: John Wiley and Sons, 1964. G.

Davenport, Elsie. *Your Handyeing.* London: Elsie Davenport. Reprint ed. Pacific Grove, California: Select Books, 1972. G.

Dendel, Esther Warren. *African Fabric Crafts: Sources of African Design and Technique.* New York: Taplinger, 1974. G.

Douglas, William O. "Journey to Outer Mongolia," *National Geographic*, March 1962. A.

Dupree, Louis. *Afghanistan*. Princeton: Princeton University Press, 1973. A.

Dye Plants and Dyeing: A Handbook. Baltimore: Brooklyn Botanic Garden, 1963. Special reprint of *Plants and Gardens*, vol. 20, no. 3. G.

Ekvall, Robert B. *Fields on the Hoof: Nexus of the Tibetan Nomadic Pastoralism*. New York: Holt, Rinehart and Winston, 1968. A.

Emery, Irene. *The Primary Structure of Fabrics: An Illustrated Classification*. Washington, D.C.: The Textile Museum, 1966. A, F.

Faegre, Torvald. *Tents: Architecture of the Nomads*. New York: Doubleday & Co., Inc., 1978. A.

"Felt," *CIBA Review* 129 (November 1958). A, C.

"Felt, A Brief Outline of the Origin, Manufacture and Uses of Wool Felt." Alhambra, California: Standard Felt Co., n.d. C.

Felt: A Mechanical and Engineering Material. Glenville, Connecticut: American Felt Company, 1951. Available at Merrimack Valley Textile Museum, North Andover, Massachusetts. C.

Felt, A Rich Tradition and Current Involvements. Detroit: Detroit Gallery of Contemporary Crafts, 1979. Catalogue of exhibit (February 17–March 17) presented by the Detroit Felt Collective. E.

"A Fiberarts Special: Dyes and Dyeing," *Fiberarts,* January/February 1978. E.

Fisher, Leonard Everett. *The Hatters*. New York: Franklin Watts, Inc., 1965. D.

Forbes, Robert J. *Studies in Ancient Technology, Vol. 4: Textiles.* New York: W.S. Heinman, 1964. A.

Gervers, Michael and Gervers, Veronika. "Feltmaking Craftsmen of the Anotolian and Iranian Plateaux," *The Textile Museum Journal,* vol. 4, no. 1 (December 1974). A, B.

Gervers, Veronika. "Felt in Eurasia," in *Yoruk: The Nomadic Weaving Tradition of the Middle East,* ed. Anthony N. Landreau. Pittsburgh: Museum of Art, Carnegie Institute, 1978. A.

Gibbs, Joanifer. *Batik Unlimited.* New York: Watson-Guptill Publications, 1974. G.

Gordon, Beverly. "Feltmaking Now: The Exciting Revival of an Ancient Technique," *Fiberarts,* November/December 1979.

Green, Louise. *Feltmaking for the Fiber Artist.* Loveland, Colorado: Greentree Ranch Wools, 1978. B.

Griaznov, M.P. "The Pazirik Burial of Altai," trans. Eugene A. Golomshtok, *American Journal of Archeology,* vol. 37, no. 1 (1933). A.

The History of Silk, Cotton, Linen and Wool. New York and New London: C.M. Saxton Agricultural Book Publishers, 1853. A, G.

Holt, Rosa Bell. *Rugs: Oriental and Occidental, Antique and Modern.* Garden City, New York: Garden City Publishing Company, 1901. A.

Hunter, Dard. *Papermaking: The History and Technique of an Ancient Craft.* New York: Alfred A. Knopf, 1943. Revised ed. 1947. Reprint ed. New York: Dover Publications, 1978. F.

Koehler, Glory Dail. "The Acid Dyes," *Shuttle Spindle & Dyepot,* Summer 1975 and Fall 1975. G.

_____. "Chemical Dyeing Preparation," *Shuttle Spindle & Dyepot,* Winter 1974 and Spring 1974. G.

Kosloff, Albert. *Textile Screen Printing.* Cincinnati, Ohio: The Signs of the Times Publishing Company, 1976. G.

Larsen, Jack Lenor and Buhler, Alfred, *et al. The Dyer's Art: Ikat, Batik, Plangi.* New York: Van Nostrand Reinhold, 1975. G.

Laufer, Berthold. "The Early History of Felt," *American Anthropologist,* New Series vol. 32, no. 1 (January–March 1930). A.

Le Coq, Albert. *Buried Treasures of Chinese Turkestan,* trans. Anna Barwell. London: George, Allen & Unwin, Ltd., 1928. A.

Levine, Louis D. "Notes on Feltmaking and the Production of Other Textiles at Seh Gabi, a Kurdish Village," in *Studies in Textile History,* ed. Veronika Gervers. Toronto:Royal Ontario Museum,1977. A, B.

McCann, Michael. *Artist Beware: The Hazards and Precautions of Working with Art and Craft Materials.* New York: Watson-Guptill Publications, 1979. G.

McClellan, Mary Elizabeth. *Felt, Silk and Straw Handmade Hats.* Doylestown, Pennsylvania: Bucks County Historical Society, 1977. D.

McFeeley, Peggy. "Tapa Design," in *Dimensions of Polynesia,* ed. Jehanne Teilhet. San Diego: Fine Arts Gallery, 1973. F.

Mattera, Joanne. "Contemporary Feltmaking," *Shuttle Spindle & Dyepot,* Spring 1976. B, E.

Meilach, Dona. *Contemporary Batik and Tie-Dye.* New York: Crown Publishers, Inc., 1973. G.

Murphy, William S. *The Textile Industries: A Practical Guide to Fibres, Yarns and Fabrics in every branch of Textile Manufacture.* Vol. II. London: Gresham Publishing Company, 1910. C, G.

Natural Plant Dyeing: A Handbook. Baltimore: Brooklyn Botanic Garden, 1973. Special reprint of *Plants and Gardens,* vol. 29, no. 2.

Naumann, W. "The Manufacture of Bark Cloths," *CIBA Review* 33 (May 1940). F.

Newman, Thelma R. *Contemporary African Arts and Crafts.* New York: Crown Publishers, 1974. G.

Olschki, Leonardo. *The Myth of Felt.* Berkeley: University of California Press, 1949. A.

Paper and Felt Redefined. Louisville, Kentucky: Louisville School of Art Gallery, 1978. Exhibition catalogue. E.

Petitpierre, A.G. "The Making of a Hat," *CIBA Review* 35 (September 1940). D.

Pope, Niran Bates. *Everybody Uses Felt: A General Description of the Origin, Structure, Evolution, Utilization, Technology and Potentials of this Natural Derivative of Wool.* New York: The Felt Association, 1950. Available at Merrimack Valley Textile Museum, North Andover, Massachusetts. C.

_____. *The Story of Felt.* Glenville, Connecticut: American Felt Company, 1946. C.

Rice, Tamara Talbot. *The Scythians.* London: Thames and Hudson, Ltd. 1957. A.

Rona-Tas, A. "Feltmaking in Mongolia," *Acta Orientalia Academiae Scientiarum Hugaricae* 16 (1963). In English. A.

Rudenko, Sergei. I. *The Frozen Tombs of Siberia: The Pazirik Burials of Iron Age Horsemen,* trans. M.W. Thompson. Berkeley: University of California Press, 1970. A.

Sommer, Elyse and Mike. *A New Look at Felt: Appliqué, Stitchery and Sculpture.* New York: Crown Publishers, Inc., 1975.

Textile Artists Newsletter, all quarterly issues from Summer 1978. Published by Straw into Gold, Oakland, California. G.

Thommen, W. "Modern Hat Manufacturing and Dyeing," *CIBA Review* 35 (September 1940). D.

Thomson, John. *A Treatise on Hatmaking and Felting (Including a Full Exposition of the Singular Properties of Fur, Wool, and Hair).* Philadelphia: Henry Carery Baird, 1868. A, D.

Trotman, E.R. *Dyeing and Chemical Technology of Textile Fibres.* London: Charles Griffin and Company, 1924. Revised ed. 1975. G.

Valentino, Richard and Mufson, Phyllis. *Fabric Printing: Screen Method.* San Francisco: Bay Books, 1975. G.

Von Bergen, Werner and Mauersberger, Herbert R. *American Wool Handbook: A Practical Text and Reference Book for the Entire Wool Industry.* Second ed. New York: Textile Book Publishers, 1948.

Von Bergen, Werner, ed. *Wool Handbook.* Vol. I. New York: John Wiley & Sons, 1963. C, G.

Wald, Pat Boutin. "Feltmaking," *Spin-off,* vol. 1 (1977). B, E.

"Waulking Songs From Barra." Notes accompanying a long-playing record published by the School of Scottish Studies. London: Tangent Record Company, 1972. A.

Wild, J.P. *Textile Manufacture in the Northern Roman Provinces.* London: Cambridge University Press, 1970. A.

Windeknecht, Margaret B. "Wool Dyed the Procion Way," *Shuttle Spindle & Dyepot,* Fall 1975. G.

Wülff, Hans E. *Traditional Crafts of Persia.* Cambridge, Massachusetts: The M.I.T. Press, 1966. A.

Index

Page numbers in italics refer to illustrations.

Edited by Michael McTwigan
Designed by Bob Fillie
Set in 10 point Times Roman